WORDS *of* WISDOM

WORDS *of* WISDOM

RAM DASS

MANDALA

San Rafael Los Angeles London

CONTENTS

INTRODUCTION

Ram Dass always had a knack for heart-to-heart transmission. Far before he had a vocabulary to describe his spiritual experiences, he lived the role of Richard Alpert, a Harvard professor experimenting with psychedelics. After these first soul-expanding journeys, he spoke and wrote about his transcendent experiences with the innate, intuitive understanding of a true inner-voyager.

Even before Richard realized that psychedelics weren't the final answer to enlightenment, he was more interested in cultivating a shared heart space with his patients and friends than he was in the clinical, scientific side of psychedelia.

I first met Ram Dass on a Skype video call in 2012, more than fifty years after his first lecture. His mode of connection had shifted, and he was already in the twilight of his life, living with the aftereffects of a stroke that permanently altered his verbal communication. He had moved into a realm that valued silence over noise—to the quiet place behind his famous words "Be Here Now"—where he rested in loving, present awareness.

During that first meeting, I told him that getting a job with the Love Serve Remember Foundation felt like an enrollment into Ram Dass College. He giggled. At the end of our conversation, after learning that I was entirely new to this world, he grinned and said, *"You're tumbling into the soup!"* Although said in jest, his proclamation became a mantra for my blossoming spiritual life. It's a reminder that I'm rarely in control, and that sometimes surrendering or, in my case, tumbling, is the only way to find even a taste of freedom and presence within the confines of our complicated human lives.

For close to ten years now, I've been in a near-constant state of immersion in Ram Dass's deep archive of teachings. I've been collecting the shiniest gems within hundreds of lectures and many hours of audio and video recordings from the last five decades—his core essential teachings—and putting them online as Words of Wisdom.

At this first anniversary of Ram Dass's passing, this anthology celebrates the spark that helped to ignite the flame of grace and Loving Awareness in so many hearts. By the end of his life, Ram Dass was a true conduit for soul connection. He wished for these five decades of teachings to find a home in an evolving world, and to serve as a beacon for the unconditional love and joy that he came to embody so deeply.

May these teachings help to walk you home.

—RACHAEL FISHER
LSRF DEVELOPMENT DIRECTOR
DECEMBER 10, 2020

CHAPTER 1

SILENCE AS THE DOORWAY

*The quieter you become,
the more you can hear.*

OPENING THE DOOR TO
THE HEART

How do you awaken out of the illusion that you are separate?

That doorway is through the heart. The heart opens a doorway into the unitive nature of the universe, and love flows through it. Love doesn't know boundaries. The mind creates the barrier of separation between you and me. The heart keeps embracing and opening out so that when you open your heart, you open into the universe to experience the preciousness, the grace, the sweetness, and the thick interconnectedness of it all.

It's beyond interconnected. It's all one thing, it just keeps changing its flow and patterns, and you're a part of it.

One of the big traps we have in the West is our intelligence. You want to *know* that you know. Freedom allows you to be wise, but you cannot *know* wisdom. You can only *be* wise. Wisdom and knowledge are two entirely different matters. Knowledge is finite and the collection of objective knowledge is a drop in the bucket compared to the ocean of wisdom.

Being wise is when you get out of the time-space locus that says, "I am the one who knows." When you merge with everything around you, you become wisdom. When you become wise, you don't know you know. You give that up. When you are wise, whatever response comes out of you is the optimum response. And at the same time, nothing is happening inside you at all.

When my guru wanted to put me down, he called me "clever." When he was praising me, he would call me "simple." The intellect is a beautiful servant, but a terrible master. Intellect is the power tool of our separateness. The intuitive, compassionate heart is the doorway to our unity.

···● ◎ ●···

The quality of the spiritual heart is that it loves without discrimination. It just loves. The mind continually sets boundaries, "This is me, this is not me, this is good, this is bad." The mind is constantly judging; the heart is not judging; the heart is just opening. The heart is without boundaries, so the mind is actually afraid of the heart.

The battle that goes on inside is interesting—you're afraid of your own heart because your heart will give away the store. The heart says, "If you need my car, if you need my house, if you need my life, take it." The mind is saying, "Now wait a minute! You've got your mortgage and health insurance to pay, keep cool, don't blow the whole scene."

The interesting question is how can you meet people in such a way that you can keep your heart open without giving up your discriminative wisdom about how to be with another person.

···● ◎ ●···

As you listen to the intuitive message of your own heart, it also reverberates through the society of which you are a part.

···● ◎ ●···

Faith is in the soul.
Belief is thought.
Faith is so rich.
Faith gives me my spiritual self.

HOW YOU GET TRAPPED IN YOUR MIND

If you keep examining your mind, you'll come to see that who you think you are and how you think it all is creates the reality you're experiencing. The illusion turns out to be the creation of the mind. The expectations of your mind create your hell.

···• ⊙ •···

When you get frustrated because something isn't the way you thought it would be, take a look at how you're thinking, not just at whatever it is that frustrates you. You'll see that a lot of your emotional suffering is created by how you think the universe should be and your inability to allow it to be as it is.

A lot of that comes from what is called "time-binding." The moment you project a future, you've trapped yourself in your mind. You say, "Well, I'm gonna get enlightened next December," which changes everything you do until then. Then in December, you're going to have to give up that model anyway. It's like those guys who said the end of the world would come. When the end of the world didn't come, they were confronted with the fact that they were caught in their own minds.

···• ⊙ •···

When you are in the moment, doing what you are doing, there is no fear. Fear comes when you stand back to think about it. The fear is not in the actions. The fear is in the thought about the actions. So how do you live in the moment, and put yourself in a position to allow "what is" to be?

Instead of sitting in expectancy, waiting for something to happen, flip it slightly and be in it. Are you really here, or are you simply waiting for the next thing? It's interesting to see where you are in relation to time—if you're always between what just happened and what will happen next, or if you are here now.

If you're feeling agitated, notice the agitation. If you're warm, be warm. If you're cold, be cold. If you're overly full, be overly full. Be it, whatever it is, but put it all in the context of a quiet space, because there's a secret in that, and it's worth playing with. There's a place where you can be inside of yourself and inside the universe, a place from which you can appreciate the delight in life. Where you can still have equanimity, quality of presence, and the quietness of peace.

···• ⊙ •···

Reflection will give you a chance to stand back in your soul, your witness consciousness, to look at your life, and see how much of the systems of which you're a part are still attractive or aversive to you. Because ultimately, the art, as Christ said, is to be *in* the world, but not *of* the world."

···• ⊙ •···

Many people look back with horror on all their past experiences and say, "Well, finally, it's getting good." That's because they haven't yet stood back far enough to see how exquisitely it all unfolds. Every confusing backtracking doubt, every fear, horrible experience, unfortunate event, pitiful circumstance, seemingly frivolous act, or sinful breakdown of discipline; every one was just a step along the path.

But to see the path, you have to be very quiet and stop thinking, because every time you think about how the path is, you create something new with that thought—even the concept of a path. You're in the moment now. This moment is the path.

INNER SILENCE

For a long time, I thought the truth had to have meaning in words, but it doesn't. Some truths are only communicated in silence. You have to figure out when to use words and when to use silence because absolute truth is silent.

···• ◎ •···

The Living Spirit, the Beloved, is always right here. It is merely your mind that prevents you from acknowledging its existence. When you quiet your mind or open your heart out so that it draws your mind along with it, only then do you rend the veil to see that the Beloved is right here.

In the Quaker tradition, the intuitive voice is called the "still, small voice within." The senses and the thinking mind are always blaring, and they have something to say about everything. To hear that little voice is a very delicate tuning, and that's part of what meditation is about, learning how to track that place inside. You listen the best you can, and then you act from the deepest place that you can hear.

···• ◎ •···

*External silence can be
the doorway to inner silence.*

···• ◎ •···

After all, you and I come here seeking truth, and the best I can understand it is that truth is not conceptual, and what you can think about isn't the ultimate truth. That's why God has no name. That's that process of getting to the place behind the form where discriminative things are unified.

····· ◎ ·····

Every religion is the product of
the conceptual mind attempting
to describe the mystery.

····· ◎ ·····

Silence is very much a part of my universe now, an awareness of silence. My universe involves using silence and not waiting for something to happen, because the silence *is* what's happening.

When you and I rest together in loving awareness, we swim together in the ocean of love. Remember, it's always right here. Enter into the flow of love with a quiet mind and see all things with love as part of yourself. Just play with the silence for a moment.

BALANCING HEART WISDOM
AND RATIONAL MIND

I'm allowing myself more and more to trust my intuitive wisdom rather than my analytic mind. My analytic mind can't really handle the complexity of the situation, so I go from moment to moment, just listening.

When you ask me a question, I stop for a moment. I go empty. I'm not thinking about the answer. I'm going empty because in the emptiness is the answer—a better response than I can come up with when I use my analytic mind to figure out what I should say to you.

What has happened to me over the past several decades, I'm sure partly through psychedelics, partly through meditation, through grace, and through evolution, is that when I don't need to think about something, my mind is empty. I'm not thinking. I'm empty. I'm just here.

···• ◎ •···

Listening is an art that comes from a quiet mind and an open heart. Listening uses all your senses, and it is a very subtle skill, not only with the ears but with your whole being. Your being becomes the instrument of listening. Your sensing mechanism in life is not only your ears, eyes, skin sensitivity, and analytic mind, but also something deeper in you, an intuitive quality of knowing. With all of your being, you become an antenna to the nature of another person. Then, for the relationship to remain a part of the Living Spirit, one of the best ingredients to put into the stew is truth.

···• ◎ •···

If you only work with your intellect and empty your mind, as in some yogas, and if you fail to open your heart, your journey becomes very dry and brittle. Ultimately, no matter your method, you have to find a balance between your energy, heart, and mind.

···• ◎ •···

In this culture, you are rewarded for knowing. It's only when you despair that the rational mind isn't going to be enough, and you see the assumptions you've been working with are not valid, that there is the possibility of change. Einstein said, "A new type of thinking is essential if mankind is to survive and move toward higher levels." He said, "Man must be able to develop a higher form of thought if he's ever going to be able to use his energy with wisdom."

···• ◎ •···

If you rest in silence,
those you meet will have
their spiritual hearts resuscitated.

···• ◎ •···

I've learned to slow down and not move as fast through things as my mind would like me to, but to feel at home in the process. See, the process and product are so interwoven that getting there is half the fun. *How* you get there is as much a part of the game as getting there.

···• ◎ •···

You and I are using words; we use speaking and listening as a vehicle for us to meet. We are capable of meeting in the intuitive heart-mind—a way of knowing one another that isn't through our immediate, analytic, intellectual process. But yet, these are word concepts that are spinning out, and you're picking them up, taking out the concepts, fitting them with your ideas, and deciding if they work for you.

You're judging by using your intellect to decide whether I'm off the wall. Am I *here*, or am I *us*, or am I *them*, or *what am I*? Whatever happened to Ram Dass? And when I share truth with the Beloved, it's a place where words are very limited, so I dance through the words with my mind while also sinking into a place of shared presence.

···· ⊙ ····

It's essential to respect the intellect, not to demean it by any means, but to realize that it has taken control when it should be a resource available for you to use when you want. You don't have to beat down your ego for God. That isn't the way it works. The ego isn't in the way; it's how you hold the ego. It is much better to do the spiritual practices and open to God and love God and trust your intuitive heart. As the transformation happens, the ego then becomes this beautiful instrument that's available to you to deal with the world. It's not in the way anymore.

···· ⊙ ····

When you develop the ego-structure—this central computer's mechanism for running the game—the question arises as to how attached you are or how identified you are with it. In spiritual evolution, you don't destroy the ego, you merely shift from identifying with it to using it as a functional unit. You still need it to function so that when I'm talking to you, I realize there's a "you" and a "me."

···· ⊙ ····

People who are enamored with their intellect don't trust the inner space. They don't know how to tune in to it. They haven't noticed its existence, because they were so busy thinking about everything. There's very little you can say to somebody going through that because it isn't real to them. It doesn't exist.

You can remind them of moments they've been out of their mind, because once you have acknowledged the existence of that other plane of reality in which you know that wisdom exists, then immediately all the moments you had in life that you treated as irrelevant or as an error, or as "I was out of my mind," suddenly become real to you. You start to trust that dimension more.

···• ⊙ •···

It's interesting that as long as you identify with your personality, the things that get you uptight are your enemies. The minute you identify with your awareness, then the things that get you uptight show you where your awareness still has sticky fingers. Because your mind deals with so much polarity, you feel that if you're happy, that means you can't be sad, so you push away what makes you sad.

But if you are going to be free, there's nothing you can turn away from or turn off. If you live fully in this moment, does this moment include that baby taking its last breath from starvation? Yes. So are you sad? Yes. Does it include the baby taking its first breath as it comes out of its mother's womb, and the joy of the beginning? Yes. So you're happy. If you are embodying the fullness of the moment, all of these are your voices. If you are to be free, there is nothing you can push away.

CHAPTER 2

TRUSTING THE
PRESENT MOMENT

*Our plans never turn out
to be as tasty as reality.*

USE EVERY MOMENT AS A
VEHICLE FOR AWAKENING

Every moment of your life, once you understand its purpose, is your vehicle for awakening. *This* moment is your vehicle for awakening. If you're uncomfortable, allow it. If you're fascinated, be fascinated. Allow it. Give it space.

···• ▣ •···

The next message you need
is always right where you are.

···• ▣ •···

You are listening as well as you can to the universe, and often you will see that when things start to happen in a certain way, your mind will focus on that because you're looking for patterns, which we call *synchronicity*. Often you will get caught in your desire to find a pattern that will give you external validation for what you're doing.

So stay with your truth from moment to moment, and get clues wherever you can. I mean, when I have a question I'll open up the *Chuang-tzu* and read something, and if it doesn't feel good, I say, "Well, that was interesting," and I close it. If it feels like what I wanted to do anyway, I say, "Oh, wow, synchronicity!" And I do it.

···• ▣ •···

So I've learned that I'm a complete phony. I might as well honor it and get on with it. You have to be very honest about your spiritual predicaments. In other words, you don't dramatically change everything once you get a new value in your head, because you're doing it with a certain attachment of mind that's going to cause you to react to it anyway. So don't get voluntarily simple too soon. Let it be something that naturally falls away, rather than you ripping it away.

····· ◎ ·····

Time is a box formed by thoughts of the past and future. Dwelling in the moment is dwelling in the soul, which is eternal presence. When you're outside of time, there's no subject or object; it's all just here. The thinking mind deals only with subject and object. But from within here and now, you watch time go by. You are not being in time. You are just being, as if you were standing on a bridge and watching time go by.

····· ◎ ·····

Learn to watch your drama unfold,
while at the same time knowing
you are more than your drama.

····· ◎ ·····

Many things can happen. You can't be afraid of making errors. You may choose the wrong teacher; you may get into a method that's no good. We all make errors. Correct them if you can, without hurting another being's spiritual opportunities. There is another rule for this game: Never use one soul for another. If your journey to God is keeping another being from going to God, forget it. You're never going to get there. It's as simple as that.

····· ◎ ·····

There was a period of time when I used to have a picture of myself on my puja table. People would come and say, "My god, what an ego this guy has." But really, it was a chance for me to practice opening my heart to myself . . . and to appreciate the predicament I am in. I mean, I could see the whole incarnation. If I am quiet enough, I can see the story line of the guy in that picture.

It's about finding a place from within yourself where you can see the unfolding of law. Dad did this; Mother did this; economics did this; education did this; opportunity did this; drugs did this; Maharajji did this.

When you look at yourself as a set of phenomena, what is there to judge? Is this flower less than that flower? It's just different. You begin to appreciate your uniqueness without it being better or worse. This is cultivating an appreciation of uniqueness rather than preference.

When someone doesn't do something that you think they ought to do, that discrepancy gets you uptight; it gets you angry or frustrated. The thing that's making you uptight is that you have a model in your head about how you think that other person should've acted. When you can look at other people's behavior and your own behavior and see the perfection in it all, you don't judge, and therefore change can occur. You're meeting the person in the place behind their behavior.

TRANSFORMING OUR REACTIVITY

We have created ecological conditions that are strangling us. Think of that: No one has done it to us—we humans have done it to ourselves.

···• ◉ •···

The minute you get near human beings, you are always saying, "You're too this," or "I'm too that." The judging mind comes in. So I practice turning people into trees, which means appreciating them the way they are.

···• ◉ •···

The universe is made up of experiences designed to burn out your reactivity, which is your attachment, your clinging to pain, to pleasure, to fear, to all of it. As long as there are places where you're vulnerable, the universe will find ways to confront you with them. That's the way the dance is designed.

···• ◉ •···

Suffering is part of our training
program for becoming wise.

···• ◉ •···

It's like a moth being drawn to light. As you reach a certain point, you realize that you only see the projections of your own mind. Everything that's happening to you is a teaching designed to burn out your "stuff." Your humanity isn't an error. All your desires are part of the journey.

You would not have taken birth on this particular plane of existence unless you had work to do in the areas of life and death—the security of your separateness, anxiety about it, lust, greed, power. Those are the prerequisites for your taking birth on this plane.

···· ◎ ····

There is no experience in your life that doesn't have the potential to liberate you. It is perfectly designed, and there is no irrelevancy in the system. When you finally want to get free, everything, every single thing in your life, becomes grist for the mill.

···· ◎ ····

When you stand back far enough, all of your life experiences are learning experiences. From a human point of view, you do your best to optimize pleasure, happiness, and beauty in life. From your soul's point of view, you take whatever comes down the pike. So from the soul's perspective, you work to get what you want, and then if you don't, "Okay, I'll work with what I've got."

···· ◎ ····

At a certain point, you realize that you see only the projections of your own mind. The projections are your karma, your curriculum for this incarnation. You are living in a universe formed from your projected attachments. That's what we mean when we say, "You create your own universe." You are creating that universe because of your attachments, which can also be avoidances and fears. As you develop spiritually and see how it all is, you keep consuming and neutralizing your reactivity more and more.

Each time you see yourself reacting, you're saying, "Right, and this situation too, and this one too. *Tat tvam asi*. And that also, and that also, and that also." Gradually the attachments start to lose their pull and to fall away. You get so that you're perfectly willing to do whatever you do, and to do it without attachment.

Everything that's happening to you is a teaching designed to burn out your attachments. Your humanity and all your desires are not errors. They're integral parts of your journey. You don't stop your desires as long as you stay in a human body. You break the identification with them. It isn't necessary to give up a thing. It's necessary to give up attachment to the thing. That's all that is required.

···• ◉ •···

From a Hindu perspective, you are born with what you need to deal with, and if you try to push whatever it is away, it's got you. You take birth as a human because you have *karma,* which is your clingings of mind. As it says in the Tao: *The truth waits for eyes unclouded by longing.* Again and again, you make decisions that end up not being in the deepest harmony with the way of things. The art of growth has to do with how quickly you admit error and start making decisions that arise out of wisdom.

HEALING THE WORLD
FROM THE INSIDE OUT

You've got to be very quiet to hear your unique *dharma*, your unique way of expression.

Somebody comes along and their primary goal in life is to regain the rights of indigenous peoples. Someone else comes along and wants to awaken people to environmental degradation. Someone else comes along and wants to stand up to the incredible oppression of women.

It isn't a question of which thing is worst, or which is more worthwhile. You have to hear what your part is and how your compassion can express itself. I am doing this gig. This is my part. It's no better than your part; it's just my part. I honor everybody's part, and I have to keep listening to hear what my part is.

····· ⊙ ·····

I do my best to give up the fruit of my actions. If I don't know what's supposed to happen, it's probably better if I don't get too attached to one particular outcome. I listen to hear what my next step should be. I act in the best way I can. And how it comes out, well, that's how it comes out. It's a matter of letting go of expectations.

····· ⊙ ·····

The real battle is with our inner feelings
and beliefs about how it ought to be.

····· ⊙ ·····

The art of playing on the playground of life is to do what you do as well as you can, while knowing that what happens is not always in your control. The key is not to be attached to the fruits of the action, even though you have worked hard for a certain result. The forces that determine whether or not you will win are not all under your control.

····◎····

People say, "What should I do with my life?" The more interesting question is, "How do I cultivate the quietness of my being, where what I should do with my life becomes apparent?"

····◎····

Don't be afraid of making mistakes. The journey is between listening to the inner voice and making a choice to take action. The minute you make a decision, if you feel it is disharmonious with another plane of existence, you must go back inside again—it's an art form of continually emptying to hear anew.

Imagine being in a relationship where two people are meeting each other anew all the time. Imagine how freeing it would be.

····◎····

The world is perfect as it is,
including my desire to change it.

····◎····

In yoga, one of the methods is contentment. That's not a goal, that's a method.

I can be content this moment, and the next moment I'm moving toward something else. When I am here, I am content. Even though I am going to change something the next minute, that doesn't mean I cannot be content with what is in this moment. That is the basis from which you do everything in yoga.

When water flows downstream, it doesn't have a model of contentment for what it is doing. It is being water, and water floats downstream because that is how water works. It is extraordinarily hard to truly realize and have sufficient faith to accept that if you stop having views, having models, planning, desiring, organizing, and structuring, it will all be alright.

···· ◎ ····

It is the continuing work of life: learning to trust that the universe is unfolding exactly as it should, no matter how it looks. You learn to appreciate that you have a part in nurturing this interconnected whole and healing it where it has torn. Discover what your individual contribution can be, then give yourself fully to it.

CHAPTER 3

CULTIVATING INTIMATE RELATIONSHIPS

It's amazing how the nature of your relationships change when it's coming out of love instead of trying to get love.

ROMANTIC LOVE AS A DOORWAY TO SOUL LOVE

The romantic quality of love between separate entities is a doorway into deeper love.

Many people experience a quality they call "love," but they're doing it with their minds, they're not really opening their hearts fully. They are *loving*, meaning "I am attracted to" or "I am attached to." When we talk about love versus fear, for example, we are talking about "being" versus "fear" or "unity" versus "separateness."

When the fear dissipates, you feel at home in the universe. Your identity with your separateness isn't overriding your feeling of connection with everything to the point that you're feeling cut off and vulnerable—where the root of the fear is. As you cultivate that unitive quality, the fear dissipates. So the relationship is between love and fear, but it's not love in the sense of "I love you"; it's the sense that we are together in the space of love.

···· ◎ ····

As long as you think of "love" as a verb, you think of it as an object. When you are in love, you are in a state of *being*.

It is entirely possible that when souls take birth (from parents that are part of their karma), they will, at some point, meet a being that they have agreed with, in advance, to do this dance together. That's what we usually call *soul mates*. But we are all "soul mates." It's not really "mates," because it's not even two.

···· ◎ ····

What you're really doing when you marry is constantly marrying yourself at the deepest level of God marrying God. A true marriage is with God. You form a conscious marriage on the physical plane with a partner to do the work of coming to God together. That is the only reason for marrying when you are conscious. If you marry for economics, if you marry for passion, if you marry for romantic love, if you marry for convenience, if you marry for sexual gratification, it will pass, and there is suffering. The only marriage contract that works is what the original contract was—you enter into this contract to come to God. That's what a conscious marriage is all about.

···• ⊙ •···

Each soul has a unique karmic predicament (you could call it a psychic DNA code) that guides how its life will go. When you begin to awaken, you do not come from such a needy place when you enter into a relationship, not looking to "lock in" so quickly. Your need is still there as a human incarnation, but you are not so identified with that need because you are already resting in a place of love.

···• ⊙ •···

You get love, it goes through you, and then you need love all over again. It's so deep in all of us that we've built a whole reality around it. You think that's the way it is—that everybody needs love and that if you don't get it you are deprived, so the more of it the better. In that sense it's like an achievement. You see people who are achievers. The minute they achieve something it becomes irrelevant and their awareness turns to the next achievement. It's because they are addicted to the practice, not to the goal.

···• ⊙ •···

The predicament with loving is the power of the addiction of the practice of loving somebody, of getting so caught in the relationship that you can't ever arrive at the essence of dwelling in love.

When you say "I'm in love with you," what you're really saying is that you are the key stimulus that is opening me to the place in myself where I am love, which I can't get to except through you.

Can you hear that one?

····· ◉ ·····

After one progresses in his or her sadhana, after meditation gets deeper, he or she lets go of the model of themselves more and more and begins to touch and enter deeper into that space of love. One begins to experience love toward more and more people. Sooner or later, you are going to be in love with the universe. You'll be sitting in that place that is love. Then when you look at another being, you are looking at love. You are in a state of love with all beings. You've given up all the stuff that's going to pull you out of this place. At this point, all of the fear in a love relationship is dissipated.

ALLOWING OUR LOVED ONES
TO BE WHO THEY ARE

One day in India, on my second stay, Maharajji said to me, "You don't have to change anybody; you just have to love them." In relationships, when the other person doesn't fit into your model of how heaven would be, you don't have to play God. You love individual differences and appreciate them the way they are because love is the most powerful medicine.

····· ◉ ·····

In relationships, you create an environment with your work on yourself, which you offer to another human being to use in the way they need to grow. You keep working. You become the soil—moist and soft and receptive—so the person can grow the way they need to grow, because how do you know how they should grow?

After a while, you come to appreciate that what you can offer another human being is to work on yourself, to be a statement of what it is you have found in the way you live your life. One of the things you will find is the ability to appreciate what is, as it is, in equanimity, compassion, and love that isn't conditional. You don't love a person more because they are happier in the way you think they should be.

What you cultivate in yourself is the garden where they can grow, and you offer your consciousness and the spaciousness to hear it.

····• ◎ •····

In your relationships, how much can you allow them to become new, and how much do you cling to what they used to be yesterday?

····• ◎ •····

When you push against somebody with even the subtlest model in your head that they should be different than they are, it awakens in them at a very unconscious level, a resistance, a subtle paranoia. And I have noticed in my human relationships that as I want less and less from each individual, there is much less pushing back from them at a deep level, and they are much more available immediately.

····• ◎ •····

The progression is quite inevitable. After some time on the path of awakening, the type of associates you share time with changes. Finally, you realize that except for existing karmic commitments—such as familial or societal obligations—there is no reason to spend time with anyone except as an aid to one's sadhana. So all new relationships— be they friendships, roommates, marriages, business partnerships— take on implicitly, and finally explicitly, this contractual basis.

When your center is firm, when your faith is strong and unwavering, it will not matter what company you keep. Then you will see that all beings are on the evolutionary journey of consciousness, differing only to the degree that the veil of illusion clouds their vision. But you will see behind the veil to the place where we are all one.

···• ◉ •···

From the soul's point of view, you come to appreciate that each one of us is living out his or her karma. We interact together, and those interactions are the grist for each other's mills of awakening. From a personality point of view, you develop judgment, but from the soul's point of view, you develop an appreciation. This shift from judging to appreciating—to appreciating yourself and your karmic predicament, and who other beings are with their own karma— brings everything into simple loving awareness.

To be free means to open your heart and your being into the fullness of who you are. Only when you are resting in the place of unity can you truly honor and appreciate others and the incredible diversity of the universe.

···• ◉ •···

I began to see that my work was purification—getting my theme straight, lightening up my attachments, simplifying my life, and relating to other human beings—so that when I met another person, I found the place in them where we are. I didn't get caught and lost in the melodrama of our relationships.

···• ◉ •···

If you're involved with relationships with parents or children, instead of saying, "I can't do spiritual practices because I have children," you say, "My children are my spiritual practice." If you're traveling a lot, travel becomes your yoga. You start to use your life as your curriculum for coming to God. You use the things that are on your plate that are presented to you. Relationships, economics, psychodynamics—all of these become grist for the mill of awakening. They all are part of your curriculum.

···• ⊙ •···

For a relationship to remain in Living Spirit, one of the best ingredients to put into the stew is truth. Gandhi spent his life in what he called experiments in truth—learning how to be straight.

RAISING FREE AND CONSCIOUS CHILDREN

If there is one thing that a person needs
from another human being, it's to be appreciated,
listened to, and heard just as you are,
not as I would make you.

···• ⊙ •···

You have to realize that your children are not containers you put things into. They are flowers that are emerging, and if you till the soil and keep it soft and fertilized, it's amazing what comes up. Inherent in all of us is profound wisdom, which gets lost in the shuffle of socialization. The question is, are you an instrument of socialization as a parent, or are you somebody that respects the inner beauty of that person, that lets the child's intuitive understanding of things lead, rather than leading out of "ought" or "should" or "must" or so on? A person learns a skill much faster when they want to than when somebody else wants them to. To that extent, you and your child are collaborative beings.

···• ◎ •···

When you give another human being, your family, or your business, the fullness of your being at any moment, a little is enough. When you provide them with half of it, because you're time-binding with your mind, there is never enough. You begin to hear the secret that being fully in the present moment is the greatest gift you can give to each situation.

···• ◎ •···

Whether you are a parent or a teacher, whatever your gig is, the only thing you can offer to another being is your consciousness. You are an environment for everyone you meet, in which they can become as conscious as they are ready to become. Offer your most conscious being to others.

···• ◎ •···

My understanding of how a child grows is that you create the garden, you don't grow the flower. You can merely fertilize the earth and keep it soft and moist, and then the flower grows as best it can. It's an interesting one because people get guilty that they're not doing enough about their children, and they tend to get caught in this sort of predicament.

You don't change your wife or your child. You keep working on yourself until you are such a clear mirror reflection, such a supportive rock of love for all those beings, that everybody is free to give up their stuff when they want to give it up—your wife's anxiety, your child's habits. You keep creating a space in which people can grow when they're ready to grow.

···• ⊙ •···

Jesus said you will get to the kingdom of God and that's where you'll find the children. I like to believe in childlike qualities as a goal, or as a way to reach spiritual awareness. It's not to go back to being a child, it's to be childlike, in the sense of innocence, openness, freshness, and beginning.

···• ⊙ •···

When you were a child, you were not taught about your Divine Self. Very few parents said, "When I look at you, I see God." What is transmitted from parent to child is all the love that can exist within the illusion, which itself is seeking the light.

At every level of the illusion there must be a total honoring of your karma, at every plane. To parents, to religion, to country, to world, to mankind, to the Divine Mother—at every level there must be honor. You can't get away with bypassing any of it, you can't leave any loose ends or they'll turn into karmic anchors.

···• ⊙ •···

You've lived your life with negative images of yourself, from childhood on, and you've built upon those images, and built upon them, and they became very heavy weights. These thoughts about you are a part of your ego, and they're manifested through your roles as child or husband, wife, breadwinner, all of those roles. They're built upon the thoughts of "I'm not truthful," or "I'm not likable" or "I'm not good"—all of those negative images.

Once you identify with your soul, you start to taste the love in your true Self, in your spiritual heart, and it's different than all of the loves you've ever had. It's just different; it's unconditional love.

CHAPTER 4

FROM BEING SOMEBODY TO BECOMING NOBODY

*Don't take yourself
so personally.*

WAKING UP TO THE ILLUSION OF OUR SEPARATENESS

As long as you have certain desires about how it ought to be, you can't see how it is.

Here in the West, we treat personality as absolutely real. For example, if you were battered as a child, it seems very real because it's a strong mental structure in your head. It permeates you, and you are your history.

At some point, you will start to see that each person is presenting who they think they are. It's like they're putting on a huge mind net, saying, "This is who I am, this is who I am . . ." You can start to see it in the way they walk, talk, dress, present themselves, always offering who they think they are, which has a historical thread running through it.

When you have started to awaken and see that there are other planes of reality that are equally valid to the one presently existing, you learn how to live with more planes simultaneously, which is what freedom is about. It's not standing in one plane; it's not standing anywhere at all.

···• ◙ •···

You are training to be nobody special. And it is in that nobody-specialness that you can be anybody.

···• ◙ •···

Which reality do you dwell in? If you stand anywhere, you're missing part of the show. Don't stand anywhere. I have no idea who you are or who I am. Then I am free. The minute I get trapped in a label, I have just imprisoned myself. No matter how well I furnish the prison, it's still a prison.

·•• ◎ ••·

There is a larger frame to the painting than the one that bounds our life's events.

·•• ◎ ••·

When you look at another person, what do you see? Body? That's desire. Personality? That's attachment. Beyond the body, beyond personality, way back in here, way back behind all the things you think you are, here we are. That's the being you serve.

·•• ◎ ••·

As I threw off my "somebody-ness," there was a different quality to the universe and myself. I could see that myself and other beings are all one, set up with different curriculums.

·•• ◎ ••·

When you say, "I am," then add anything after it, you are already trying to stand somewhere. There's nowhere to stand in this whole dance. You can't stand somewhere when you say, "I am good." There is stuff in you that isn't so good. You say, "I am young," yet get old. "I am alive," yet you will be dead. Every definition of yourself is a prison you put yourself in, seemingly to protect yourself. But it ends up creating anxiety and fear. Most of the behavior that our society performs is motivated by fear of what is.

·•• ◎ ••·

Your ego is a set of thoughts that define your universe. It's like a familiar room built of thoughts; you see the world through its windows. You are secure in it, but to the extent that you are afraid to venture outside, it has become a prison. Your ego has you conned. You believe you need its specific thoughts to survive. The ego controls you through your fear of loss of identity. To give up these thoughts, it seems, would annihilate you, so you cling to them.

There is an alternative. You needn't destroy the ego to escape its tyranny. You can keep this familiar room to use as you wish, and you can be free to come and go. First, you need to know that you are infinitely more than the ego room by which you define yourself. Once you know this, you have the power to change the ego from prison to home base.

···• ◙ •···

I am still a person with an ego, and there is a little bit of stuff in which I'm somebody. So I'm in training to become nobody. And this is my training field, right here. I have to sit day after day with hundreds and thousands of people looking up at me, like this, saying "yes, oh yes, oh Ram Dass yes, oh yes, ah thank you, ah Ram Dass." That is my fire. It's all those mind nets saying, "This is who you are, this is who you are."

If I get stuck in being the actor of somebody who's doing good, watch it! Then my mind creates a reality in which everybody that comes into my mind field is somebody for whom good needs to be done. It's so seductive to get caught in roles. We can play the roles, but let's not get stuck in them.

···• ◙ •···

We are addicted to power because of separateness—separate nations, separate states, separate religions, and separate people. When you are separate, the whole universe is powerful, and you are so little.

When you get into your soul, the entire world is made of love—trees are made of love; beings, in their souls, are made of love.

·•• ⊙ ••·

Most of us stay locked in our separateness, very frightened of coming out of it. You feel very vulnerable. In truth, you are not vulnerable at all, but you think you are vulnerable. That's what Christ was repeatedly saying, but nobody seemed to want to hear him. It's tough to open your heart when you are not vulnerable.

When you are in the presence of unconditional love, that's the optimum environment for your heart to open because you feel safe. You realize nobody wants anything from you. The minute the heart opens, you are once again letting in the flow, and that flow is where you experience God.

·•• ⊙ ••·

In most of our human relationships, we spend much of our time reassuring one another that our costumes of identity are on straight.

·•• ⊙ ••·

The root of fear is the feeling of separateness within the model one has of oneself. Once that feeling of separation exists, then you process everything from that model. It then keeps reinforcing the sense of vulnerability, because there are incredibly powerful forces moving both inside and outside of you.

The transformative process of spiritual work is reawakening to the innocence of going behind that model of separation that one has, that cuts you off, that made you a tiny little fragile somebody. A lot of the power comes from a freeing of your fragility.

BEING PRESENT AND OPEN-HEARTED IN OUR DAILY ROUTINES

As we grow in consciousness, there will be more compassion and more love, and then the barriers between people, between religions, between nations will begin to fall. We have to beat down the separateness.

···• ◎ •···

Treat everyone you meet like God in drag.

···• ◎ •···

Most means of gaining livelihood do not, in and of themselves, increase the illusion of separateness. When you are involved in such vocations, then it is your work on yourself which makes the particular occupation a vehicle for bringing people out of illusion and into yoga.

As you progress with your sadhana, you may find it necessary to change your occupation. Or you may find that it is only necessary to change how you perform your current occupation to bring it into line with your new understanding of how it all is. The more conscious a being becomes, the more they can use any occupation as a vehicle for spreading light.

···• ◎ •···

Christ said to be *in* the world, but not *of* the world. You are simultaneously living your story line—keeping your ground, remembering your zip code—yet still having your awareness free and spacious, not caught in anything, delighting in the richness of this timeless moment.

·· •• ⊙ ••· ·

If I am in my soul, when I look at others, I see their souls. I still see the individual differences—men and women, rich and poor, attractive and unattractive, and all that stuff. But when we recognize each other as souls, we see each other as aspects of the One. Love is the emotion of merging, of becoming One. Love is a way of pushing through into the One.

·· •• ⊙ ••· ·

To bring to our daily life a quality of awareness, an openheartedness, a consciousness that understands the interrelationship of all things, means that you can begin to hear how you can live on Earth in harmony with all things.

·· •• ⊙ ••· ·

When you're identified with awareness,
you're no longer living in a world of polarities.
Everything is present at the same time.

·· •• ⊙ ••· ·

Every teacher, every life experience, everything you notice in the universe, is but a reflection of your attachment. If there is nothing you want, then there is nothing that clings, and you go through life free, collecting nothing.

You collect a sight, you collect a record, you collect a computer, you collect a relationship, you collect a teacher, you collect a method—more clinging. Use them all. Be with them. Enjoy them. Live fully in life. But don't cling. Flow through it.

As you are quiet and listen and hear how it all is, you will relate to all of it in a harmonious way, in a way in which there is no exploitation. Harmonious in how you relate to the floor you're sitting on, to the person next to you, to the night air, to the world you live in.

···· ◎ ····

People think, "Oh, you're being here now, so you're not responsible," in the sense that responsible means time-binding over past and future. However, all the past and future, everything you always were and will be, is in this moment; all of your commitments for the future are in this moment. The fullness of this moment includes everything. It does not exclude the past or future.

All you're dealing with is the problem that the human mind clings, and the clinging of the human mind takes it into time and space. It takes away from the fullness of the moment. The most exquisite practice becomes something like the practice of Vipassana meditation, in which you keep extricating yourself from identification with thoughts about past and future, noting them and then coming back to the present moment, to the breath, which is right here. It becomes easy.

···· ◎ ····

What I used to do when I had to wait in line was mantra or breathing. I'd go into my Vipassana meditation. But now I'm interested in whether waiting in line at the bank can itself be the thing. I notice my impatience, notice the feeling in my feet as I'm standing there, notice the different levels of reality of the people I'm looking at. Am I seeing a bank teller, or am I seeing the Divine Mother as a bank teller? I allow myself to play with the moment more, dealing with the stuff of the moment rather than going away.

···• ◎ •···

In India, when we meet and part, we often say *namaste*, which means: I honor the place in you where the entire universe resides; I honor the place of love, of light, of truth, of peace. I honor the place where, if you are in that place in you and I am in that place in me, there is only one of us.

···• ◎ •···

If you live in the moment, you are not in time. If you think, "I'm a retired person. I've retired from my role," you are looking back at your life. It's retrospective; it's life in the rearview mirror. If you're young, you might be thinking, "I have my whole life ahead of me. This is what I'll do later." That kind of thinking is called time-binding. It causes you to focus on the past or the future and to worry about what comes next.

Getting caught up in memories of the past or worrying about the future is a form of self-imposed suffering. Either retirement or youth can be seen as moving on, time for something different, something new. Aging is not a culmination. Youth isn't preparation for later. This isn't the end of the line or the beginning. Now isn't a time to look back or plan ahead. It's time to be present. The present is timeless. Being in the moment, being here with what is, is ageless, eternal.

CENTERING OURSELVES TO FEEL AT HOME IN THE UNIVERSE

When fear dissipates, you feel at home in the universe, meaning your identity with your separateness isn't overriding your feeling of connection with everything to the point that you're feeling cut off and vulnerable, which is where the root of fear is. As you cultivate that unitive quality, the fear dissipates. The relation is one between love and fear, but it's not love in the sense of "I love you"; it's the sense that we are together in the space of love.

···• ⓞ •···

I'm home because I'm a soul.

···• ⓞ •···

There is no "them" in the universe, there is only "us." We as a collective must purify ourselves. Each individual must hear her or his *dharma*; that is, how their manifestation must come forth to relieve suffering in whatever form it takes. Until you are enlightened, it must be an exercise in working on your own consciousness.

···• ⓞ •···

A moment comes when "other" is no longer other.

···• ⓞ •···

There is grace in your life, but you have to have faith to see it. It's a contract between God and the individual: grace on one side, faith on the other.

···• ◎ •···

There's a place that you can be inside of yourself, inside of the universe, in which you can appreciate the delight in life. Where you can still have equanimity, and quality of presence, and the quietness of peace.

Imagine a mandala or a flower, and think about the center of the flower and all the petals that come out from the center. Think of the center of the flower as absolutely still, and think of all of the petals as moving, as energy and change.

Where is your center?

···• ◎ •···

Through an open heart,
you hear the universe.

···• ◎ •···

One day I was sitting in a motel in Middle America, one of those plastic Holiday Inn–type places. I went into my room, sat down and set up my little puja table, moved the menu and all that stuff, and it was kind of depressing. I thought, "Well, a few more weeks and I'll be done with this tour, and I can go home." Then I saw the pain that thought created in me.

I got up, walked out of the room, closed the door, walked down the hall, turned around, came back, unlocked the door, and yelled, "I'm home!" I came in, sat down, and looked around. I thought, "I wouldn't have decorated this way particularly, but what the hell. You know, if I'm not at home in the universe, boy, I got a problem."

What is home? Home is where the heart is. Home is the quality of presence. It's the quality of being wherever you are.

····● ⊚ ●····

We're all just
walking each other home.

CHAPTER 5

GIVING FORM TO THE FORMLESS— ON GOD AND GURU

Each of us has God within.

"SUB EK" (ALL ONE)

Maharajji often repeated, *Sub ek!* ("It's all One!") He had a gesture in which he would hold up his index finger, almost in admonition, as if to say, "Can't you see it's all One?" Buddha, Christ, Moses, and Krishna are all just different aspects of the same being.

···• ◙ •···

The essence of my relationship with Maharajji is to love him, open myself to his presence, and surrender to him. That's my bhakti practice, a practice of guru kripa. The qualities of love and openness and surrender are the essence of every bhakti practice.

You find some being that draws your heart—Maharajji or Anandamayi Ma, Christ or Krishna, Allah, or God. You pick the name. Then you invite that being in. You install that being in your heart, and offer yourself to it: Sing to it, chant to it, pray to it, bring it flowers. You love, and you open. And then you watch as, slowly but surely, you love your way into becoming it.

···• ◙ •···

There is a being on another plane that guides, protects, and helps you. That loves you so incredibly. Does your sense of unworthiness prevent you from being loved as much as this being loves you? Unworthiness has to go. You have to be able to say, "Christ, God, Baba, let me feel your love. Let me fill up with your love, let me be absorbed into your love."

Breathe in and out of your heart. With each inhalation, you take in that love a little more. With each exhalation, you get rid of that which keeps you from acknowledging that you are love.

···• ◎ •···

Inspiration is God
making contact with itself.

···• ◎ •···

I have always said that often the religion you were born with becomes more important to you as you see the universality of truth.

WHAT THE GURU GIVES YOU

I had a moment with Maharajji when I was sitting across the courtyard from him while he was talking to a group of people, and I was watching everybody fawn all over him, asking questions, and I thought, "What a bunch of crap. What am I doing here? I don't care if I ever see this guy again." And I felt immediately guilty about the thought.

Maharajji turned, looked over at me, grabbed this old fellow, whispered to him and sent him running across to me. He bent down and touched my feet, and said, "Maharajji said, 'Ram Dass and I understand each other perfectly.'"

···· ⊙ ····

My relation to Maharajji has gone way beyond the romantic quality of guru. I mean, that's not really what the issue is between us anymore. We share a space of presence that is very soft and liquid, but it isn't romantic. It isn't very emotional anymore. It's just presence together.

···· ⊙ ····

My path is the path of *guru kripa*, which means "grace of the guru." It seems like a strange path in the West, but my path involves my relationship with Maharajji, Neem Karoli Baba. The way I do that is, I hang out with him all the time. I have an imaginary playmate in a way. I mean, he's dead, he dropped his body, yet he seems so alive to me because I have invested that form in my mind with an emotional connection to that deeper truth.

For me, Maharajji is the cosmic giggle. He is the wisdom that transcends time and space. He is an unconditional lover. He is the total immediate presence.

···· ⊙ ····

Maharajji is as available to you as he is to me.
You can have him as a friend, and you can
use him as a mirror for what's inside you.

·•·• ◉ •·•·

It's very hard to open your heart to another being whose love is conditional. They're saying, "I will love you as long as you're a certain way," so you keep protecting yourself. You find it very easy to open yourself to inanimate objects, or an animal, or a memory, or to a very young child. A child is innocent before it develops any definition of itself and starts to manipulate the universe to get what it needs.

When you're with a guru, the guru doesn't need you to do anything. They just need you to be who you are. Their love is unconditional, and when you're in the presence of unconditional love, that's the optimum environment for your heart to open.

·•·• ◉ •·•·

Most of the beings that we call gurus are really teachers. The likelihood of finding somebody that's a cooked goose is reasonably slim. Since they are not cooked geese, they have their own karma, they have their own stuff. So they become somebody through whom a teaching comes, but they themselves are not the truth.

If there is purity in your heart in the way you see truth, you separate the purity of their message from the stuff of their karma. You take the truth, and you work with it.

HONORING THE GURU
IN US ALL

Everybody you know, you see, you remember, you will meet, is another face of God, another doorway through. It is another way that God has come to you to awaken your attachments, bring them to the forefront, and allow you to see through them.

···· ⊚ ····

When you know how to listen,
everybody is the guru,
speaking to you.

···· ⊚ ····

The next true being of Buddha-nature that you meet may appear as a bus driver, a doctor, a weaver, an insurance salesman, a musician, a chef, a teacher, or any of the thousands of roles that are required in a complex society—the many parts of Christ's body. You will know him because the simple dance that may transpire between you—such as handing him change as you board the bus—will strengthen your faith in the divinity of humans. It's as simple as that.

···· ⊚ ····

When you learn to honor everybody you meet as your teacher, you'll see that there is nothing else you can do but be conscious, for the good of yourself and your fellow men and women. You begin to see that everything in your universe becomes your teacher, so your teacher is everywhere. You don't have to rush to India because it's always right where you are. Some beings can get as high as any enlightened being ever got while sitting in the middle of Topeka, Kansas, or the middle of New York City, or anywhere. It depends on your readiness, and that has to do with your karma and your willingness to get on with it.

···• ◉ •···

Can you imagine how different life would be if it were to start from total fulfillment—how many of your actions would be different if you already were that which you seek to become? In truth, as the Buddha said, "All beings are the Buddha."

···• ◉ •···

I honor the light in all of us. The more I love God, the more I love God's forms, which are all forms. Living from the soul is very much a heart-centered journey. I get on a bus, and by the time I get off, I feel like I have intimately met family members I've known all my life. We're all in love with one another. To live in your spiritual heart with the degree of openness it entails, trust in the One. In that loving awareness, you are not as vulnerable as you would be in the ego, where you think you are separate from others.

···• ◉ •···

You couldn't possibly be lonely, because where could you go? Do you think if I go to the bathroom and lock the door, I can be alone? I can't be. The living spirit, the community of our consciousness, that guru inside, is always one thought away.

···• ◉ •···

Surrender to the One. Surrender to your *atman*, because you have the One inside of you. That means you don't surrender to the God with a beard, you surrender to the God inside. My relationship with Maharajji is an inside job. Once he left his body, I could very much identify him inside of me, and I would surrender to that voice inside. That voice is joyful, compassionate, loving, peaceful, and wise. I find it very enjoyable to surrender to that God inside. If you shift your identification into the atman, you will see what the world looks like to the One. It's quite different than the world you perceive through your ego. It's a fun thing to surrender.

···· ◎ ····

The quickest way through your stuff is to learn how to listen inside. The inner guru is always there for you once you recognize it. You must honor your own path. You must be able to trust that there is a place in you that knows what is best. There is a tendency to look to others for guidance. Only you know what is suitable for you. Trust your intuitive heart. When it speaks, listen. If it feels "right on," do it.

···· ◎ ····

Ramana Maharshi said that God, guru, and the Self are the same. The guru, the true guide, awakens our own deeper being, or atman, which is God itself. Ramana Maharshi realized that Self directly. His view from the Arunachala mountain, his darshan, his teaching, pointed directly at the atman, at Self-realization.

That unity of God, guru, and Self is the higher truth, and if your veil of attachment is very thin, you may be able, like Ramana, to penetrate directly to that essence in the heart. But most of us, to get through our busy human incarnation and the profusion of forms we find in our lives, need guidance and help. Seeing the guru as separate from yourself is a way to approach it in steps of lesser truths. It's a first step toward becoming the One.

The guru's guidance as separate from yourself is a method or vehicle for coming to God. It's using a relationship with a separate entity, dualism, to get to the One, to the reality that the guru is identical with your innermost being.

CHAPTER 6

RELEASING OUR MODELS OF SPIRITUAL GROWTH

You can't push yourself into enlightenment. You can only wait for grace.

LETTING GO OF THE MODELS OF WHO YOU THINK YOU ARE

It's very hard to grow because it's difficult to let go of the model of yourself in which you've invested so heavily.

· · • ⊙ • · · ·

Individual differences are not better or worse, merely different. If you forgo judging, you come to understand that each of us has a unique predicament that requires a unique journey. While we share the overall trip, your particular experiences are your own. No set of experiences is a prerequisite for enlightenment. People have become enlightened in all ways. Just be what you are.

· · • ⊙ • · · ·

Of course, it's embarrassing not to be infinitely wise, but I feel that what we can offer each other is our truth of the growing process, which means we fall on our faces again and again. Sri Aurobindo says, *"You get up, you take a step, you fall on your face, you get up, you look sheepishly at God, you brush yourself off, you take another step, you fall on your face, you get up, you look sheepishly at God, you brush yourself off, you take another step . . ."* That's the journey of awakening.

If you were awakened already, you wouldn't do that, so my suggestion is you relax and don't expect that you will always make the wisest decisions. Realize that sometimes you make a decision and, if it wasn't the right one, you change it.

· · • ⊙ • · · ·

When you stop living by other people's judgments or expectations, you start doing what you need to do. In trying to decide what you want to do with your life, listen to your heart. The program is much farther out than you ever thought it was. I never thought I'd be a yogi. Each of us has our unique karmic predicament, our individual work to do. Always choose that which you feel is most in harmony with the way of things.

····· ◎ ·····

The melodrama of fanaticism is a form of spiritual materialism: you make spiritual life into something else to acquire, like a new car or television set. Just do your practices; don't make a big deal out of them. The less you dramatize, the fewer obstacles you create. Romanticism on the spiritual path is just another attachment that will have to go sooner or later.

····· ◎ ·····

When you first understand there's a journey, a path, you tend to get somewhat hysterical. You want to sell it to everybody, change everybody, and whichever path you buy first, you try to convert everybody to it. The zeal is based on your lack of faith, because you're not sure of what you're doing, so you figure if you convince everybody else . . .

But you're moving into a new space. You're finished with the first wild hysteria, and settling down into the humdrum process of living out your incarnation as consciously as you know how to do. If in the course it turns out this is your last round to get enlightened, fine. If not, that's the way it is. There's nothing you can do about it. You can't bulldoze anybody to beat the system—you are the system. The desire to beat the system is part of it.

····· ◎ ·····

Over the years, you develop strong habits of perceiving the universe, and you come to be very secure within these habits. You selectively perceive your environment in ways that reinforce your habits. This collection of habits is what we call "ego." But meditation breaks the ego down. As you begin to see through the ego, you can become confused as to what reality is. What once seemed absolute now begins to seem relative.

When this happens, some people get confused; others fear they may be going insane. The best strategy for dealing with this disorientation is to note it and let it be. The path to freedom is through detachment from your old habits of ego.

Slowly you will arrive at a new and more profound integration of your experience in a more evolved structure of the universe. That is, you will flow beyond the boundaries of your ego until, ultimately, you merge into the universe. Until then, you must break through old structures, develop broader structures, break through those, and develop still broader structures.

···• ◙ •···

It's only when caterpillarness is done that you become a butterfly. That is part of this paradox. You cannot rip away caterpillarness. The whole trip occurs in an unfolding process over which you have no control.

···• ◙ •···

It's as if you are born into a spacesuit that allows you to function on this plane. You spend many years learning how to operate the suit, and the superstructure of the suit is the ego. Most people forget that they were born into the suit and that they are not actually the suit.

THE IMPORTANCE OF WITNESSING YOUR THOUGHTS

My strategy is to keep cultivating the witness, that part of me that notices how I'm doing. I cultivate the quiet place in me that watches the process of needing approval, of the smile on my face, of the false humility, of all the horrible creepy little psychological things that are just my humanity—and I watch them occur again and again and again.

·⋯• ◉ •⋯·

One part of getting free, free into the soul or the witness, is the ability to stand back a little bit because now you are identified with being the witness rather than being the player, and thus you can see the play more clearly.

·⋯• ◉ •⋯·

The first step of karma yoga is to get free of the attachments to your own life and develop a witness. You have thousands of *me's,* and there is one "me" that watches all the other me's. That's the only game. It's not trying to change any of the me's.

·⋯• ◉ •⋯·

The witness is not the evaluator, it's not the judge, and it's not the superego. It doesn't care about anything. It just notes, "*hmmm,* there he is, doing that again." That witness, that place inside you, is your centering device. And that begins to be the work one does on oneself.

The witness is part of your soul. It's witnessing your incarnation, this lifetime, from the heart-mind. It's the beginning of discrimination between your soul and your ego, your real Self, and yourself in the incarnation. Once you begin to live in this witness place, you begin to shift your identification from the roles and thought-forms. As you witness yourself, the process becomes more like watching a movie than being the central character in one.

···• ⊙ •···

There's an interesting series of stages in karma yoga, the yoga of living daily life as an exercise in becoming pungent, where you develop a witness—a place in yourself that watches your whole melodrama, your dance. It doesn't judge you; it doesn't try to change you; it's not trying to become enlightened. It's just watching the whole thing. Ultimately you live simultaneously in all of the planes of consciousness so that, in a way, it's like a vertical cutup—you look at somebody, they're there/they're not there.

···• ⊙ •···

There are ways of subjectively being in the universe so that things are available to you, or in you, that would otherwise only be knowable to you by collecting them through your senses and through your thinking mind. If you were to take your consciousness and bring it out of your senses and out of your thinking mind and bring it down into awareness, what then? Who would you be? Just awareness or consciousness.

···• ⊙ •···

The technique of the witness is to merely sit with the fear and be aware of it before it becomes so consuming that there's no space left. The image I usually use is that of a picture frame and a painting of a gray cloud against a blue sky. But the picture frame is a little too small. So you bend the canvas around to frame it. But in doing so you lost all the blue sky. So you end up with just a framed gray cloud. It fills the entire frame.

So when you say "I'm afraid" or "I'm depressed," if you enlarged the frame so that a little blue space shows, you would say, "Ah, a cloud." That is what the witness is. The witness is that tiny little blue over in the corner that leads you to say, "Ah, fear."

···• ◎ •···

Who you think you are will always be frightened of change. But it doesn't make any difference to who you truly are.

···• ◎ •···

If there is anything at all that can bring you down, if your house is built on sand and there is fear, you aren't free. For where there is fear, you are not free. Thus you become motivated to confront the places in yourself that bring you down; not only to confront them, but to create situations in which to bring them forth into light.

···• ◎ •···

When people say, "may peace be with you," peace cannot be with the ego, except for the briefest second. That's because the ego's made up of stuff that doesn't allow for it. And the soul is still moving toward something, toward awareness. Awareness is peace.

ADAPTING TO CHANGE AND MAKING MISTAKES WITHOUT SELF-JUDGMENT

You should feel no guilt about where you are in your spiritual path. Wherever you are—be it at the beginning of the journey, well on your way, or resting comfortably at some height—you must acknowledge where you are, for that is the key to further growth.

You should keep some perspective about the entire journey so that you will not sink into complacency, feeling you have finished the journey when you have not even begun to approach liberation.

···• ⊙ •···

The spiritual journey is individual, highly personal.
It can't be organized or regulated.
It isn't true that everyone should follow one path.
Listen to your own truth.

···• ⊙ •···

I think everyone that wants God thinks it's a continuing possibility that they will get through in this lifetime. However, you can only go at the rate you can go, and when you're done, you're done. The only thing you can ask is that you keep awakening at the fastest rate at which you're capable. You can't go any faster than that, and whether you think you're going to make it in this lifetime or not doesn't really make a difference, as long as you keep going full blast.

···• ⊙ •···

The truth is everywhere. Wherever you are, it's right where you are, when you can see it. And you can see it through whatever vehicle you are working with; you can free yourself from certain attachments that keep you from seeing it. The scientist doesn't stop being a scientist, no one stops being anything. You find how to do things that allow you to see truth of where you are at the moment. I'd say you never find out anything new; you just remember it.

·••• ◉ •••·

The art of growth has to do with how quickly you admit error. We always make decisions from where we're sitting; then that decision leads to a new moment, and then in the new moment you listen again, and often you realize that the new moment suggests that the previous decision just led you into a new moment in which there is another decision that isn't going to be consistent with the last one.

To the extent that you keep coming back into the existential situation with the trust that if you keep listening to the moment, and keep being true to what you hear, while people may be upset with you because you are not consistent, you will stay as close to the truth as you hear it. That's what you can offer the universe.

·••• ◉ •••·

The first rule: listen to your inner voice. Second rule: be honest with yourself. The predicament is that you listen to your inner voice and it leads you to a path, and then you outgrow it. You don't want to admit that you've outgrown it because you've made a big investment in it. But you must be willing to let go and stand as naked as a newborn child, again and again.

·••• ◉ •••·

How stable is anybody's life? When stability is threatened, people contract. If you've got an investment, and then it all starts to change and you can't quite stop it, you contract, your heart closes, you go up into your mind. When you get into your mind, you cause a lot of trouble. In the service of fear, the mind causes the quality of the thinking to become about things, so it sees everything as an object. All people become "them," and "they" must be dealt with.

···• ◉ •···

You and I are in training to find a place in ourselves and the way we live our lives, where we don't freak out about changes to our dependent form of existence—a place where we don't freak out in the presence of change or increasing chaos.

The root of the problem lies in the way we deal with change. Most of us feel so insecure that we want to create a structure around us that makes us feel safe, and then we don't want it to change. Any change increases our uncertainty and our confusion and our inadequacy . . . and it frightens us. Think of how bizarre that is, because you are a part of nature. Look out there and show me something that isn't changing. The nature of things is that they change, including us. Do you see how you're in a losing strategy if you pit yourself against change?

···• ◉ •···

Did you ever have a bad day? Everything seems to go wrong, and you are completely lost in anger, frustration, and self-pity. It gets worse and worse, until the final moment when you have just missed the last bus. There is some critical point where it gets so bad that the absurdity of it all overwhelms you, and you can do nothing but laugh. At that moment, you uplevel your predicament; you see the cosmic joke in your suffering.

Humor puts things in perspective. There are many levels of humor—the humor of survival, the humor of sex and gratification, the humor connected with power. Beyond all these, there is a humor that is filled with compassion. It is reflected in the tiny upturn in the Buddha's mouth, for he sees the humor in the universal predicament: All beings are lost in illusion, yet he knows that they will awaken from that illusion for they are, at heart, already enlightened. He knows that what seems so hard for them is, from another perspective, their path to liberation.

···• ◎ •···

When you have your game all together,
and there is still a yearning inside of you,
and you say, "I don't understand
why I'm still unhappy, I've got it all."
Well, that yearning is your ticket
to spiritual awakening.

···• ◎ •···

In mystical traditions, it is one's readiness that makes experiences easily understandable or esoteric. The secret isn't that you're not being told; the secret is that you're not able to hear.

CHAPTER 7

FINDING FREEDOM THROUGH SPIRITUAL PRACTICE

*There is no best or right kind of experience
in meditation; each
session is as different and unique
as each day of your life.*

HOW MEDITATION CAN BE INTEGRATED INTO DAILY LIFE

In the clarity of a quiet mind, there is room for everything that is happening, and whatever else might also be possible.

As we've discovered, it is possible to notice a single thought, sensation, or situation arise, but not get lost in identifying with it. You observe the cloud but remain focused on the sky, see the leaf but hold in vision the river. You are that which is aware of the totality. And your skills develop with practice.

First, you have to appreciate the value of such qualities of mind and desire to develop them. Next, you have to have faith in the possibility that you can indeed make progress. Finally, you have to explore and practice appropriate techniques. Twenty minutes per day of such practice can lead to results and the incentive to go deeper still. Continuous practice brings about great transformation of mind and leads to a new quality of service.

···• ◉ •···

If you meditate regularly, even when you don't feel like it, you will make significant gains, allowing you to see how your thoughts impose limits on you. Your resistances to meditation are your mental prisons in miniature.

···• ◉ •···

Meditation provides a deeper appreciation of the interrelatedness of all things and the part each person plays. The simple rules of this game are honesty with yourself about where you are in your life and learning to listen to how it is.

Meditation is a way of listening more deeply, so you hear exactly how it is from a deeper space. Meditation will help you quiet your mind, enhance your ability to be insightful and understanding, and give you a sense of inner peace.

···· ◎ ····

When meditation works as it should,
it will be a natural part of your being.
There will no longer be anything apart
from you to have faith in. Hope starts
the journey, faith sustains it, but it
ends beyond both hope and faith.

···· ◎ ····

If you have ideas of what should happen, you can become needlessly disappointed if your meditation doesn't conform to these expectations. At first, meditation is likely to be novel, and it's easy to feel you are changing. After a while, there may be fewer dramatically novel experiences. The changes you undergo in meditation are often too subtle to detect accurately. You may be making the most progress when you don't feel anything particularly significant is going on.

Suspend judgment and let whatever comes come and go.

···· ◎ ····

I don't want you to do your practices because they ought to be good. I want you to do your practices like you go to the toilet. You don't go to the toilet because you're good; I mean, you know why you go to the toilet. That's the way spiritual practices should be done.

It's an excellent advertisement for spiritual practice: *Come spend the weekend with spiritual practices. It's like going to the toilet!*

···· ◎ ····

Learn how to be comfortable with aloneness and do not define it as loneliness. Realize that while your incarnation, your ego, is a socially derived construct, your soul is not. Your meditation practice is done to bring you back into your soul identity, where you can recognize that we are all alone, but you're only lonely if you're caught down in ego.

···· ◎ ····

The final step in integrating meditation into your awareness is to use the stuff of daily life as part of your meditation. There are ways of perceiving the world and the way you live in it, such that each experience brings you more deeply into the meditative space.

At the same time, however, this kind of meditation requires firm grounding: you must continue to function effectively in the world as you meditate on it. This is meditation in action. It finally becomes the core of a consciously lived life, a meditative space within you. This space stands between each thing you notice and each response you make, allowing a peaceful, quiet, and spacious view of the universe.

NAVIGATING THE UPS AND DOWNS OF SPIRITUAL PRACTICE

The transformation that comes through meditation is not a straight-line progression. It's a spiral, a cycle. My own life is very much a series of spirals in which, at times, I am pulled toward some particular form of *sadhana* (spiritual practice) or lifestyle and make a commitment to it for maybe six months or a year. Then I assess its effects. At times I work with external methods, such as service. At other times the pull is inward and I retreat from society to spend more time alone. The timing for these phases in the spiral must be in tune with your inner voice and your outer life.

Don't get too rigidly attached to any single method. Turn to others when their time comes, when you are ripe for them.

···• ⊙ •···

Are all methods to be avoided? It doesn't seem so. But it does seem useful to see them in perspective. Methods are ships crossing the ocean of existence. If you're halfway across the sea, it's a little silly to decide methods are a bummer if you don't know how to swim; but once you get to the far shore, it would be silly to keep carrying your boat because there is no more water.

The game seems very simple: Methods are not the thing itself; methods are traps. You use methods, and you entrap yourself to burn out the things that keep you from being free. Ultimately the methods spew you out at the other end, and the method disintegrates into nothingness. Every method. The guru, chanting, study, meditation, practices, all of it. The end result is nothing special.

···• ◎ •···

You start doing chanting as a technique. You begin to sing, *Shri Ram, jai Ram, jai jai Ram.* You start thinking it means, "Honorable Ram, hail Ram, hail hail Ram." After an hour, you stop thinking about all of that, and you are just singing. You realize the aesthetic of the music and how beautiful it is. After a while, it starts to go deeper until your heart is singing; it's singing from inside you. Then there's a point where true *bhakti* starts—dualism ends and you become like the chant. You are in a space where it's not emotional anymore. It's moved into a deeper, intuitive quality of love. Touching that love leaves you with trust in the method and confidence in where it takes you—trust in the Beloved and trust in how you get there.

SIMPLIFYING YOUR LIFE TO SUPPORT YOUR JOURNEY

Meditation helps other parts of your life become simpler. As you enter quieter spaces, you will see how clinging to desires has made your life complicated. Your clinging drags you from desire to desire, whim to whim, creating more and more complex entanglements. Meditation helps you cut through this clinging.

If, for example, you run around filling your mind with this and that, you will discover that your entire meditation is spent letting go of the stuff you just finished collecting in the past few hours. You also notice that your meditations are clearer when you come into them from a simpler space. This encourages you to simplify your life.

···• ◎ •···

The more I center myself and meditate, the more I hear how it all is. Even if I don't understand how it all is, the more *I am* how it all is. If there's an uneven place in me, all I have to do is work on myself. As I give up attachment to knowing how it all works, the actions come into harmony with the Tao.

···• ◎ •···

Every moment a thought enters your mind, right at that moment, before the seed takes root, offer it. You can offer it to *Kali Ma*, to *Christ*, to me, it doesn't matter. Offer it to God, like you are full of opening, full of God, full of the Living Spirit.

Meditation raises the question, "Who am I really?" If you think you are the same as your ego, if you open up the ego's filters and overwhelm it, you will be drowned. If, on the other hand, you are not exclusively what the ego defines you to be, then removing the ego's filters may not be such a great threat. It may actually mean liberation. But as long as the ego calls the shots, you can never become other than what it says. Like a dictator, it offers you paternalistic security at the expense of your freedom.

You may ask how you could survive without your ego. Don't worry—it doesn't disappear. You can learn to venture beyond it, though. The ego is there, as your servant. Your room is there. You can always go in and use it as an office when you need to be efficient, but the door can be left open so you can always walk out.

···· ⊙ ····

If you feel free only when you meditate, you're not really free. Freedom does not come from turning your back on your responsibilities. The game is to be in the world, but not of it. Even when you find yourself feeling spaced out, disoriented, or not together, you can make an extra effort to meet the needs of the moment, whether it's the baby's diapers that need changing or your income tax that's due. Don't make meditation a cop-out from life.

···· ⊙ ····

As you observe the patterns of your thoughts during meditation, notice which areas of your life keep cropping up as distracting thoughts and pulling on you. You will quickly see what you must clean out of your closet to proceed more smoothly.

For example, if you have heavy debts, and thoughts about these debts intrude when you meditate, rather than accrue more and more debts as our society urges, you will find yourself wanting to lessen them. As you simplify things like your finances, you clearly see how the laws of cause and effect work in your life.

You will want to get your life lighter and clearer so that there are fewer expectations upon you from all quarters. Later, when your meditative center is strong, you can carry many responsibilities without clinging to your thoughts.

···· ⊙ ····

Though you can start meditation any time, it's harder if your life is chaotic, if you're feeling paranoid, overwhelmed with responsibilities, or sick. But even starting under these conditions, meditation will help you to clear things up a bit. Slowly you reorganize your life to support your spiritual journey.

At each stage, there will be something you can do to create a supportive space. It may mean changing your diet, who you're with, how you spend your time, what's on your walls, what books you read, what you fill your consciousness with, how you care for your body, or where and how you sit to meditate. All these factors contribute to the depth and freedom that you can know through meditation.

····· ◉ ·····

The trap of high experiences, however they occur, is that you become attached to their memory and so you try to recreate them. These memories compel you to try to reproduce the high. Ultimately they trap you because they interfere with your experience of the present moment.

In meditation, you must be in the moment, letting go of comparisons and memories. If the high is too powerful compared to the rest of your life, it overrides the present and keeps you focused on the past. The paradox, of course, is that were you to let go of the past, you would find in the present moment the same quality that you once had. But because you're trying to repeat the past, you lose the moment.

····· ◉ ·····

For many of us who have come into meditation through psychedelics, the model we had for changing consciousness has been "getting high." We pushed away our normal waking state to embrace a state of euphoria, harmony, bliss, peace, or ecstasy. Many of us spent long periods getting high and coming down.

My guru said, "These medicines will allow you to come and visit Christ, but you can only stay two hours. Then you have to leave again. This is not the true samadhi. It's better to become Christ than to visit him—but even the visit of a saint for a moment is useful." Then he added, "But love is the most powerful medicine." For love slowly transforms you into what the psychedelics only let you glimpse.

AT THE PEAK OF THE MOUNTAIN, ALL PATHS COME TOGETHER

Once you are starting to awaken, you look around for practices to purify and help you awaken. Most people see meditation as this practice. It's a clear and simple yoga, and you say, "Well, while I do yoga, I do my meditation, and then I go to work," or "then I live life," or "then I'm gonna do good," or something like that.

Karma yoga is taking all of the "good or something" that you are going to do after your meditation, and making those all into an offering and practice of awakening.

It's a perspective, an attitude that one has, an attitude of offering, and an attitude of seeing how the actions you are performing are much more.

···· ⊙ ····

I do my spiritual practices because I do my spiritual practices. What will happen will happen. Whether I will be free and enlightened now or in ten thousand births is of no concern to me. What difference does it make? What else do I have to do? I cannot stop anyway, so it does not make any difference to me. But one concern is to watch that you do not get trapped in your expectations of practice.

There is a great delight in tuning into a variety of different methods and looking to each method to move you in its unique way and keep opening you. So be very generous in your opening to methods, because if you bring a pure heart and a yearning to be free, they will serve you in that way.

How do you get your "karmuppance" with methods? If you use them for power, you get power. Then you are stuck with the power. If you use them to reinforce your separateness, you get left in your separateness.

···• ◎ •···

Practices of purification are done in order to "cool out," so you're not creating so much heavy karma for yourself. We are always preoccupied with the creations of our minds. What you strive to be liberated from is your habitual thought patterns and the pull of your senses. Lightening up in these areas gives you the space to refocus and deepen the benefits of centering the mind with meditation, mantra, or the practices of *bhakti* yoga. With the deepening of these practices comes higher wisdom.

···• ◎ •···

When most of us think of yogis, we think of somebody sitting, like Milarepa, up in a cave in the mountains, cross-legged and naked. There was snow, and ants were eating him, and the only food he took was nettle soup, and he ate it for so long he developed a green nettle fur all over him. But he was busy freeing himself to come into union. Now that kind of moratorium is pretty unrealistic for most Westerners, so what role does yoga play in the West for us at the moment?

Well, along the way it will teach you how to control your consciousness, calm your mind down, find a center, and get your body into harmony with your thoughts. It will get you back far enough inside yourself so that you can start to see how it all is, and start to experience compassion for yourself and for others around you.

····◎····

When I asked Maharajji how to meditate, he said, "Meditate like Christ." I said, "Maharajji, how did Christ meditate?" He became very quiet and closed his eyes. After a few minutes, he had a blissful expression on his face, and a tear trickled down his cheek. He opened his eyes and said, "He lost himself in love."

····◎····

My route is through the heart of devotion.
That is a path. There are many pathways here.
One is the path of wisdom, one is the path
of calming the mind, one is the path of
opening the heart. Mine is the path of love.

····◎····

What I have come to understand is that my path involves my heart. It can't go after the fact. It has to be the leading edge of my method. And in a devotional path, you work with forms to transform your own identities. In the process, you break the habits you've held as your reality and your self-definition. And the new realities, the new concepts you take on, because they were taken on intentionally, don't have the same hold over you that the old ones had. It's using a skillful means to get rid of one thing when later you will get rid of that aid as well.

···· ◎ ····

The devotional path isn't necessarily a straight line to enlightenment. There's a lot of back and forth, negotiations if you will, between the ego and the soul. You look around at all the aspects of suffering, and you watch your heart close in judgment. Then you practice opening it again and loving this, too, as a manifestation of the Beloved, another way the Beloved is taking form.

Your love grows vast. In bhakti, as you contemplate, emulate, and take on the qualities of the Beloved, your heart keeps expanding until you see the whole universe as the Beloved . . . even the suffering.

···· ◎ ····

Ramakrishna said, "Only two kinds of people can attain self-knowledge: those whose minds are not encumbered at all with learning—that is to say, not overcrowded with thoughts borrowed from others—and those who, after studying all the scriptures and sciences, have come to realize that they know nothing."

That last part is when the *jnana* yoga path is working because the "know nothing" is the next step in this trip. You learn and you learn until you realize that you don't know anything with all you've learned—and that's the route through. You use your intellectual models to get you going—they're really helpful for that—but you don't cling to the models; you keep letting go of them, letting go of the intellectual structures. Otherwise, they get in your way.

···· ◎ ····

In religious study, while there is the opening for healthy skepticism, there is another way to open Pandora's box and let it all in. Figure that whatever is supposed to be useful to you, you will hold, and whatever else will fall away. You don't have to keep it all away at arm's length for fear you will lose your virginity or something. You don't have to protect your purity against the holy books. You open up and let it come in, no matter how weird it all seems.

·· • ◎ • ··

The Indian saints Kabir and Tulsidas, as well as St. Theresa, showed an incredibly intense yearning and love for God. On the other hand, Ramana Maharshi taught the path in which the discriminative mind, through the method of self-inquiry, extricates one from clinging, even to the concept of "I." Others, such as the Tibetan sages Padmasambhava and Milarepa, embodied the skillful use of tremendous powers in humanity's service. Jesus reflected the purest love, compassion, and sacrifice. Buddha showed the path of insight. All these are different routes to a single goal of liberation.

There are many, many paths to the mountain top. Each has its unique sights, experiences, and hazards. Don't get stranded along the way.

·· • ◎ • ··

Miracles and gatherings of *satsang*, reading or hanging out with holy books, chemicals, they're all traps, but they are useful because they keep strengthening your faith. Faith can touch that place inside, which is called the *atman*. It's naive to think that any one route will bring you faster than any other route other than what is supposed to be your route. In Zen, they say, "The journey of a thousand miles begins with the first step."

Your work on yourself starts where you are at this moment. If you're thinking about the future or the past, if you're planning, if you're collecting this for later, what about right here? Now. This is what it's all about. Everything you've ever done in your life and all your incarnations are for this moment.

···• ◎ •···

I've found that each meditation technique I've ever pursued has helped me by touching another space in my being. Somehow I've danced through them without getting caught in a value system that would say that a single meditative technique is the only way. You cannot, however, keep collecting methods all the way to enlightenment. Sooner or later, you will be drawn to one path or another, which is for you the eye of the needle, the doorway to the inner temple.

···• ◎ •···

The journey passes from eclectic sampling to a single path. Finally, you recognize the unity of your own way and that of other seekers who followed other paths. At the peak, all the paths come together.

CHAPTER 8

GETTING FREE FROM SUFFERING

*If you think you're free,
there's no escape possible.*

USING OUR SUFFERING AS A VEHICLE FOR AWAKENING

Suffering is a lesson the soul needs to get to its Beloved. Joy is too.

When I look back on the suffering in my life—this may sound strange—but I see it now as a gift. I would have never asked for it for a second. I hated it while it was happening, and I protested as loudly as I could, but suffering happened anyway. Now, in retrospect, I see how it deepened my being immeasurably.

···· ◎ ····

Within the spiritual journey, you understand that suffering becomes something that has been given to you to show you where your mind is still stuck. It's a vehicle to help you go to work.

···· ◎ ····

Both Hindus and Buddhists say human birth is highly auspicious because it has the elements for liberation. You have everything you need to work within a human birth to become realized: consciousness or awareness, conceptual understanding, the emotional heart, joy, and sorrow.

When Buddhists talk about the preciousness of a human birth, it's the awareness associated with human birth that's the opportunity. You become aware to bring yourself to higher consciousness. Suffering is part of it, too; it's all grist for the mill of developing awareness. What's here in front of you is what you can be aware of; it's food for enlightenment. It's your part in this passing show of life.

···• ◎ •···

When you realize you want to relieve suffering, you realize that you have to become an instrument for the removal of suffering, and that means you have to be free of suffering. Then there is the choice: to deny suffering or to change yourself inside.

···• ◎ •···

You are moving toward
a light that embraces the darkness.

···• ◎ •···

I deal with the immensity of suffering by cultivating more than one plane of consciousness and acknowledging the laws of the universe. When I arrive at a perceptual vantage point where I look at a leaf, or a drop of water, or stars and planets, I see the extraordinary, exquisite, and awesome nature of the lawful relationships of phenomena.

I can find the universal laws in physics, astronomy, music, genetics, mathematics, in chemistry, in each field I examine. From that perceptual vantage point, I cannot help but be filled with awe at the magnificence of how it all works. And I realize that the way it all works includes suffering.

···• ◎ •···

Your suffering tells you where your mind is clinging. If I experience suffering from aging, it's because I have a model of myself that's other than what this is. This is what this is, including dying, pain, loss, all of it.

The models in our heads about it and how we cling to it are the root of suffering. So when you want to get free badly enough, you begin to experience your suffering as grace. You don't ask for it. You don't say, "Give me suffering," but when it comes, you see it as something that shows you a place where you are holding. It shows you the place to release.

We're not talking about the renunciation of external actions. We're talking about renouncing attachment to them, to your melodrama. It is your attachments to your melodrama that keep you from being here now. Appreciate them, but don't get caught in them. Don't take your melodrama so seriously. Remember who you really are, which is a soul, not ego.

····◉····

You are continually going to sleep and waking up. All you can do is keep searching for the clarity and quietness amidst the confusion of your melodramas.

····◉····

As the Tao says, "Truth waits for eyes unclouded by longing." But we often don't hear the truth fully because of the clinging or attachment of our minds; we only hear the projections of our desires. Again and again, we make decisions that end up not being in the deepest harmony with the way of things. Working through an attachment means you have to work with that desire until you are no longer attached to that desire. The desire may go on, but you are no longer attached to it.

····◉····

The offering up or cleaning up of ego stuff is called purification, the act of letting go. This is done out of discriminative awareness. That is, you understand that you are an entity passing through a life in which the entire drama is an offering for your awakening. You see that the life experience is a vehicle for coming to God, for becoming conscious, for becoming liberated. And you understand ultimately that's what you are doing here.

···• ◎ •···

The most exquisite paradox: As soon as
you give it all up, you can have it all.
As long as you want power, you can't have it.
The minute you don't want power, you'll
have more than you ever dreamed possible.

···• ◎ •···

Sometimes you experience a quality of dying or emptiness about life. It's scary because you built your whole game up—you saved all your money to buy a Mercedes-Benz. Then you buy a Mercedes-Benz, and after about a week, it's just another car. How can it be just another car when you spent years buying a Mercedes-Benz? There's a real horror when meaningful stuff becomes meaningless—and you are awakening.

···• ◎ •···

The truth is that behind the drama, here you are, no matter how poignant, captivating, dramatic, or bittersweet it may be. Your work is not to get snared in anybody else's or your own drama.

Can you accept total suffering, take on the karma of another human being, and yet not be attached to the melodrama of suffering? If a person is suffering, the only thing you can do for them is to find the place in them which is behind suffering. It's all you can do. It's all that's available.

WORKING WITH OUR EMOTIONAL SPECTRUM AS GRIST FOR THE MILL OF AWAKENING

*The beginning of wisdom comes
from the capacity to look at what is.*

···• ⊙ •···

For respect to come to you, you must respect yourself first. And for you to respect yourself first, you've got to make contact with that part in you that is worthy of respect. Not your will, but a deeper part of your being.

···• ⊙ •···

As I have explored my own and others' journeys toward love, I've encountered different types of happiness. There's pleasure, there's happiness, and then there's joy. Addiction, even in the broad sense of just always wanting more of something, gives only pleasure.

Pleasure is very earthbound when you're getting it from sensual interaction, and it still has its opposite—the need for satisfaction is never-ending.

Happiness is emotional, and emotions come and go. It may play into the complex of other emotional stuff that we all carry. But there is also spiritual happiness, which gets very close to joy. As it becomes less personal, spiritual happiness becomes joy. Joy is being part of the One. It's spiritual, the joy-full universe, like trees are joyful. It's bliss or *ananda*. It's all those things. The difference is that it comes from the soul.

···• ⊙ •···

In working with your emotions, there is meditation for quieting down and seeing how lost you've become. On the deeper devotional path, there is offering the emotion to God or guru, saying, "Here, you take it, I offer it to you." Appreciate your humanity—*Yeah, here I am, I just lost it again. Ah, so. Right. Okay.* It's the ability to see it without denying it. Saying, "I am upset. Far out. Here we are again." It is like talking with God and saying, "Look how deliciously human I am."

···• ⊙ •···

Surrender who you think you are and what you think you are doing into what is. It is mind-boggling to think that spirituality is dying into yourself.

···• ⊙ •···

The game of powers is always very simple: Don't use them. The minute you get power and say, "I've got this power, I will use it," you're stuck again: a new attachment, a new ego trip. Don't use them; instead, let them be used through you.

Purity is one of the lions at the gate that brings you incredible powers. The minute you're a little less attached than everybody else, you have incredible power over everybody, because you don't want anything that everybody else wants so much. The minute you don't want so much, suddenly you're free in a way you can't believe because you're so used to being trapped in this network of needs and desires.

···• ⊚ •···

Try to cultivate a spaciousness or an awareness around emotions like anger and sadness that allows you to acknowledge the feelings. It comes back to the word "appreciating." Acknowledge the feelings and allow them, and see them as part of the human condition. They're all generated—they're subtle thought-forms—and they all arise in response to something. If someone does something, you have a certain emotional response, a certain reactive domain that you get into.

You're cultivating a quietness in yourself that watches these things coming and going and rising and passing away. You learn not to act out your emotions, but to appreciate and allow them. That's part of how you use them spiritually. Spiritually, you don't act them out; you just acknowledge them. You don't deny them, though. You don't push them down. You acknowledge that "I'm angry," but you don't have to say, "Hey, I'm angry!" That's the key.

So in devotional practices, you aim emotions towards God. For the other kinds of emotional realms, you witness them, and you sit with them, watch them change and come and go, and don't deny them; you allow them because that's part of your human condition.

···• ⊚ •···

When you talk about service, you'll see that it awakens intense emotions, and you have to let your heart break. But you've cultivated another plane of reality, which is the one that notices and allows it: a quality of equanimity that lies within it.

•••• 🔘 ••••

You go from using the spiritual journey
in service of your psychodynamics to using your
psychodynamics in service of your spiritual journey.

RESPONDING TO CHANGE WITH LOVE INSTEAD OF FEAR

In the late '60s we had the Vietnam and anti-Vietnam forces in this culture that were destabilizing. What happens in the presence of that destabilization, where there is human unconsciousness, is that people get frightened. When they get frightened, they use certain mechanisms: They go into denial, they become more fundamentalist, they try to find values they can hold on to to ward off evil. They cling and become ultranationalist. There's more ethnic prejudice, racial prejudice, and anti-Semitism. It all increases, because this fear isn't just in us; it's a common thing.

These changes are happening very rapidly. People respond with fear, and you must ask yourself the question: Is there any place you can stand inside yourself where you don't freak out? Where you can be quiet enough to hear the predicament and find a way to act that is at least not contributing to the further destabilization?

•••• 🔘 ••••

You and I are in a situation of very dramatic change, and the interesting question is how you respond to change, whether it's in your own body or in the social structures you're in. What happens when the family breaks down? When the government isn't functional? When your IRA isn't as good as it was? Feel the chills run through you.

It's interesting to look at whether change is your friend or enemy, and whether you can find a place in yourself from which you can see phenomena changing without being trapped in the fear generated by being identified with that which changes.

···· ⊙ ····

If I can't stop thinking, maybe I can let my thoughts go by without getting caught up in them. Feel the breeze on your face or your neck? See how it's going by? You're not all hung up with it. You don't have to see where each breeze goes. You don't have to glance to see if it hit those trees over there. It's breezes, and they're just going by. Make your thoughts like those little breezes, just going by.

···· ⊙ ····

You get to be at home with change and uncertainty. You get to be at home with not knowing how it all comes out. You make a plan knowing full well that it may be irrelevant a moment later, and you're at peace with that.

I find that when I'm at a choice point, the best thing to do is to be quiet and empty and go back to square one. But I try to stay at the choice point as long as I can, because that's as interesting a place as any other, to stay with not knowing what to do. But if you listen, it all becomes apparent in time. Patience is good—the tolerance for not knowing what's what is quite an art form.

FINDING FREEDOM THROUGH EMBRACING OUR HUMANITY

As long as we grab at our divinity and push away our humanity, we aren't free. If you want to be free, you can't push away anything. You have to embrace it all. It's all God.

···• ⊙ •···

As I have gone from identity with ego to identity with soul or witness, I have found a space in relation to the mystery of the universe that allows me to be with the suffering that lives on this plane in a way that doesn't overwhelm me. I'm not overwhelmed by my impotence to take it all away and I don't have to look away from it. I deal with it as it arises.

···• ⊙ •···

There is a tendency in us to find suffering aversive, to distance ourselves from it. Like if you have a toothache, it becomes that toothache. It's not us anymore. It's that tooth. If people are suffering, you want to look at them on television or meet them but keep a distance from them, because you are afraid you will drown in it. You are afraid you will drown in a pain that will be unbearable, but the fact of the matter is you have to. You finally have to, because if you close your heart down to anything in the universe, it's got you. You are then at the mercy of suffering.

And then having finally dealt with suffering, you have to consume it into yourself. This means you have to—with eyes open—be able to keep your heart open in hell. You have to look at what is and say, "Yeah, right." It's bearing the unbearable. And in a way, who you think you are can't do it. Who you really are can do it. So who you think you are dies in the process.

·••• ◉ •••·

We can take our lives exactly as they are in this moment. It is a fallacy to think that we're necessarily going to get closer to God by changing the form of our lives, by leaving so-and-so, or changing our jobs, or moving, or by giving up our stereos, or cutting off our hair, or growing our hair, or shaving our beards.

It isn't the form of the game; it's the nature of the being that fulfills the form. If I'm a lawyer, I can continue being a lawyer. I merely use being a lawyer as a way of coming to God.

·••• ◉ •••·

You can't push away the world.
You have to enter into life
fully to become free.

·••• ◉ •••·

People often say to me, "I would really like to do *sadhana* (spiritual practice), but now I'm a teacher. If I could only finish being a teacher, I could do sadhana." Baloney! You're doing sadhana or you're not. Sadhana is a full-time thing because there is nothing else to do. You do it whether you're teaching or sitting in a monastery, whether you're lying in bed, going to the toilet, making love, or eating.

Everything is part of waking up. Everything is done without attachment. Another way of saying it is: It's all done as consecrated action. It's all dedicated. It's all sacred. How can you live in the moment if you are too busy warding off what is? What is, is the suffering inherent to being human. You must accept the fact that your heart is breaking all the time.

···• ⊙ •···

Being peacefully in relationship to everything made me realize that my happiness isn't based on the situation being "this way" or "that way"—my happiness is one that embraces my sadness. My love is one that embraces my hate.

···• ⊙ •···

To be free, it's not enough to have tasted
emptiness; we have to reintegrate that,
so our every act is empty yet compassionate.

···• ⊙ •···

If you're going to give up desires, what desire do you use to give up desires? You use the desire to offer it all in sacrifice. All of it, even the desire to make the sacrifice, becomes the sacrificial offering. That's the return to the roots, spiritualizing life through offering up all your acts as the sacrifice for your transformation. You sacrifice the ego's goals and the ego's point of view. You throw every part of yourself into the fire.

Swaha! Take it, God. Just let me be free.

CHAPTER 9

LOVING OUR DARK THOUGHTS

Your problem is you are too busy holding onto your unworthiness.

ACCEPTING OURSELVES AMIDST OUR NEUROSES AND IMPERFECTIONS

Cosmic humor, especially about
your own predicament,
is an important part of your journey.

•••• ⊙ ••••

Many people try to counteract the "I am not good enough" with "I am good enough." In other words, they take the opposite, and they try to invest it, which still keeps the world at the level of polarities. The art is to go behind the polarities. So the act is to go not to the world of "I am good" to counteract "I am bad," or "I am lovable" as opposed to "I am unlovable," but go behind it to "I am." "I am" includes the fact that I do crappy things, and I do beautiful things, and I am.

•••• ⊙ ••••

We all love our own melodramas. We each have one. Everybody thinks they're somebody doing something, or somebody thinking something, or somebody wanting something. We all get so involved in our melodramas, so busy thinking we're the actors, so busy thinking we're doing it all—and it's really just this lawful stuff running off. How funny!

But in order to see that, to begin to appreciate the lawfulness of the unfolding, you need to develop a little perspective. It can be a nice meditation to take a seed and put it in a bit of earth. Put it on a kitchen window sill, and watch it grow into a plant, into a flower. Just observe it every day. Use that as your daily meditation exercise—see the way the whole process unfolds.

···• ◉ •···

Let's trade in all our judging
for appreciating. Let's lay down
our righteousness and just be together.

···• ◉ •···

WORKING WITH NEGATIVE EMOTIONS: LUST, ANGER, CONFUSION, AND GREED

We have all been enchanted with getting high and having free awareness, and so we have tried to repress or deny lows when our awareness once again gets caught in this or that. We love the illusion of being high, but are afraid of coming down.

As your journey proceeds, you realize that you can't hold on to your highs and deny your lows. Your lows are created by the remaining attachment that blinds your awareness. Facing your lows—your anger, loneliness, greed, fears, depressions, and conflicts—is the most productive fire of purification you can find.

···• ◉ •···

Once you get a taste of the freedom that comes with letting go of your stuff—anger, righteousness, jealousy, your need to be in control, the judging mind, to name a few—you start to look at those things in new ways. That is the teaching of being in the moment for someone who understands that this precious birth is an opportunity to awaken, is an opportunity to know God. All of life becomes an instrument for getting there—marriage, family, job, play, travel, all of it. You spiritualize your life.

····◉····

When I start to get angry, I see my predicament and how I'm getting caught in expectations and righteousness. Learning to give up anger has been a continuous process. When Maharajji told me to love everyone and tell the truth, he also said, "Give up anger, and I'll help you with it."

Maharajji offered me a bargain: "You must polish the mirror free of anger to see God. If you give up a little anger each day, I will help you." This deal seemed more than fair, and I readily accepted. And he's been true to his end of the bargain. I found that his love helped to free me from my righteousness. Ultimately I would rather be free and in love than be right.

····◉····

You and I are not only here in terms of the work we're doing on ourselves. We are here in terms of the role we're playing within the systems we are a part of. If you look at how change affects unconscious people, you can see how change generates fear; fear generates contraction; contraction generates prejudice, bigotry, and ultimately violence. You can watch the whole thing happen, and you can see it happen in society after society. The antidote for that is a consciousness that does not respond to change with fear. That's as close to the beginning of that sequence as I can get.

···• ◉ •···

You've got to remember that the ego is built on fear; it's not built on love. It's built on fear of nonsurvival, so you create a structure to make you safe. It's a beautiful instrument, but if you're identified with it, you're fearful all the time. You're fearful, so you're always going to overcompensate and make ego decisions that are a little inappropriate because they'll be colored by your looking from inside this place.

When you're outside of it, you see that you use your ego as you need to make decisions. You come back into somebody-ness. You and I are meeting behind this dance that we're doing, which is charming and fascinating. That's the beauty of playing with the ego and the higher consciousness. It's only when those two planes work that the ego becomes functional.

···• ◉ •···

You want to get to the place where, when there is depression, instead of running and hiding from the depression, trying to grab at the next high, you turn around. You look at the depression as though you were looking the devil in the eye, and you say to the depression, "Come on, depression, do your trip, because you're just depression and here I am."

···• ◉ •···

You can't mask impurities for very long. When you suppress or repress them, they gain energy. Eventually, you have to deal with your same old karmic obstacles. Maharajji used to enumerate them with regularity: *kama, krodh, moha, lobh*—lust, anger, confusion, and greed. It's the spectrum of impulses and desires that condition our interior universe and our view of reality.

You have to take care of this stuff so you can climb the mountain without getting dragged back down. This clearing out opens the door for dharma, for being in harmony with the laws of the universe on both a personal and social level. If you do your dharma, you do things that bring you closer to God. You bring yourself into harmony with the spiritual laws of the universe. Dharma is also translated as "righteousness," although that evokes echoes of sin and damnation. It's more a matter of clearing the decks to be able to do spiritual work on yourself.

····· ◎ ·····

If you follow your heart, there is nothing to fear. As long as your actions are based on your pure seeking for God, you are safe. Any time you are unsure or frightened about your situation, there's a beautiful and powerful mantra: "The power of God is within me. The grace of God surrounds me," which you can repeat to yourself. It will protect you. Experience its power from above the top of your head down to the base of your being. Grace will surround you like a force field.

CHAPTER 10

SERVING OTHERS WITHOUT GETTING LOST IN SEPARATENESS

If you would truly bring peace
to the world, identify with that
place within you where you
are peace.

BECOMING AN INSTRUMENT
OF SOCIAL CHANGE

I have three major instructions for my life from my guru: love, serve, and remember. Love everyone, serve or feed everyone, remember God.

In all cases, it's my work on myself, because I am loving, serving, and remembering, but what I love and serve is a function of what I remember. What I remember is who we all are. I remember the Self—and that remembering means that my love and service towards another being are directed towards the place in them that is already free.

••• ◉ •••

As long as you think you're somebody who's doing something, you're lost in the illusion and can't offer anyone else the space to extricate themselves from their negative reality. You must come to see every human being, including yourself, as an incarnation in a body or a personality, going through a particular life experience. You allow it to be just the way it is now, seeing even your confusion and conflict and suffering as functional rather than as dysfunctional.

••• ◉ •••

Work to extricate yourself from the illusion of your separateness, and then do what you do in life. And as you do what you do in life, if you're a shoemaker you make shoes, if you're a mother you raise your children; whatever you're doing, that is the vehicle through which you express that.

It's like C. S. Lewis saying you don't see the center because it's all the center. Whatever you are is the center of the whole game, and it resonates out from there. A fully conscious bus driver can affect everybody in the traffic around them, and everybody that steps on their bus.

···• ◎ •···

There is a way of shifting consciousness so that you see that you're one in the form of many. You understand that a starving person or a dying person or a frightened person is you. Then the whole trip of, "What's good for me? What do I want? What do I need?" becomes less interesting. And that changes the universe.

···• ◎ •···

Do what you can on this plane to relieve suffering by working on yourself to be an instrument for the cessation of suffering. To me, that's what the emerging game is all about.

···• ◎ •···

In your daily life, how do you become an instrument of social change? You become in yourself the statement of love, the statement of choiceless awareness, you become the moment so that your presence liberates everyone that comes near you if they are ready. You do nothing to anybody. You live your life.

Which life do you live? Whatever your dharma demands. If your work is to protest the injustice of racism, you protest. If your work is to raise a family, you raise a family. If your work is to be a good lawyer, you're a good lawyer. If your work is to meditate in a cave, you meditate in a cave. No blame, no reward. You do your dharma.

···• ◎ •···

You don't need to wait until you are enlightened before you act in the world, and you don't need to withdraw from the world to become enlightened. Conscious social action can be your work on yourself that becomes the vehicle for your awakening.

···• ◎ •···

The curriculum of *seva* (service) provides you with information about your strengths, and you discover how these contribute to genuinely helpful service. Each time we drop our masks and meet heart to heart, reassuring one another simply by the quality of our presence, we experience a profound bond that we intuitively understand is nourishing everyone.

Each time you quiet your mind, your listening becomes sharp and clear, deep and perceptive; you realize that you know more than you thought you knew, and can reach out and hear the heart of someone's pain, as if from inside. Each time you can remain open to suffering, despite your fear and defensiveness, you sense a love, which becomes increasingly unconditional.

AVOIDING THE TRAP
OF RIGHTEOUSNESS

Don't get caught in righteousness; don't get caught in helping somebody. It doesn't mean you don't help them; just don't get caught in it. If you really want to help somebody, instead of ripping off the experience of helping them for yourself, give up helping anybody. Then just be with them and see what happens.

· · • • ◎ • • · ·

The final act of service is to acknowledge and honor another being's integrity as they, like you, pass through the beauty and pain of a human birth. Its immediate meaning may surpass your understanding, but you are willing to keep the faith, which St. Paul describes as "the evidence of things unseen." Ultimately, all is well.

· · • • ◎ • • · ·

If you are to help heal the world, you need to remember that it is sacred. Your actions need to be positive statements, to remind you that even in the worst times, there is a world worth struggling for. You need to find ways to keep the vision alive, acknowledge but not get caught in the dark side, and remember that even the worst aspects of suffering are only part of the whole picture. You need to enter lightly.

· · • • ◎ • • · ·

You can heal my soul
if your heart is a mirror for my soul—
and your heart can be that mirror
only if you are resting in your own soul.

···· ⊙ ····

I want to play the part of someone who has worked on my consciousness sufficiently so that if things get tough, in terms of environment, social structures, oppression, minority groups, whatever the situation is—I would like to be able to be in the scene without getting caught in my own reactivity to it, without getting so caught in my own fear that I become part of the problem instead of part of the solution.

···· ⊙ ····

It's quite apparent that as you work on yourself, on your consciousness, and continue to do whatever dance you're doing, the dance evolves. You begin to see how the acts you perform can become more and more optimal to the conditions. For instance, when you're about to change a law in a country, you begin to understand how the whole system works. You see what the optimal act you can do is, and you perform it totally, without emotional attachment to that act, and instead have an awareness of how that act works in the whole system.

It's the ability sometimes to have a delay of gratification and the ability to stand back to do what is the more optimal response.

···· ⊙ ····

Grace is something that an individual can see about their own suffering and then use to their advantage. It is not something that can be a rationalization for allowing another human being to suffer.

···· ⦿ ····

You have to listen to the level at which another person is suffering.

When somebody is hungry, you give them food. As my guru said, "God comes to the hungry person in the form of food." You give them food, and then, when they've had their belly filled, they may be interested in questions about God.

Even though you know from, say, Buddhist training, or whatever spiritual training you have had, that the root cause of suffering is ignorance about the nature of dharma. Giving somebody a dharma lecture when they are hungry is just an inappropriate methodology in ending suffering.

···· ⦿ ····

You can't say, "I'm not going to have anything to do with politics." You can say it, but you've got to watch where you're saying it from. You may say, "I'm not going to get involved with politics because I am so busy with something else, and I'll vote, but I'm not going to put my time into campaigning for candidates and things like that, or issues, because my energies are best used here." That's fine.

If you've thought it through and felt that way, you can look somebody in the eye and say, "This is the way it is." But if you're saying, "I do not have anything to do with politics because it's too dirty and because I don't approve of it," forget it—you are abdicating your responsibility to society. It's as simple as that.

···· ⦿ ····

We're at an interesting moment within the shift of collective consciousness, specifically around how we're integrating the changes in power structures. Now business holds sway over government, over religion, in terms of social power. And business is like pirates on the high seas. The question is, do you control it from the outside or does it control itself? Does the whole process have a meta game that's controlling itself, and can you stand back far enough to see how it's playing out? How is the shift in collective consciousness going to evolve and what part do you play?

Part of the curriculum is looking at the systems that you are a part of and saying, "That system needs work." It's essential to be able to shift your game so that you're not merely pushing the system away and saying, "I don't think about that stuff, because it's too complicated. Let somebody else worry about it." Because as long as you get frustrated with the system, you may be standing in the way of everybody's survival.

RADIATING TRUTH AS A WAY TO SERVE OTHERS

I'm explicitly making my life a teaching by expressing the lessons I've learned so it becomes a map for other people. Everybody's life can be like that if they choose to make it so, choosing to reflect on what they've been through and share it with others.

···· ⊙ ····

As you get more conscious, every act you perform increases the amount of consciousness in the universe, because the act itself conveys the consciousness. In other words, I could tell you the greatest truths of the world, but if I don't understand them inside myself, forget it—because I'm not giving you the key that allows you to use it, which is the "faith" in it, which I can only convey through my success in whatever I'm doing.

···• ⊙ •···

Truth is one of the vehicles for deepening spiritual awareness through another human being. If there is a license for that in the relationship, in any relationship—with a guru, with a friend, with a lover, with whatever it is—it is an optimal way of coming into a liquid spiritual relationship with another person. But it's very, very delicate because you feel very vulnerable. You have parts of your mind that are cut off, and the idea that's been socialized is, "If I show this part of me, I will not be acceptable." Until finally, you risk making your truth available.

So truth is one of the exciting vehicles to work with in a relationship. What I've learned is to use my lecturer role to make my truth as available as possible. I find that people say, "Thank you for being so truthful. It makes it easier for me to be truthful about myself because you've done that." I think well, it's a cheap price to offer yourself up for that purpose if it begins to help other people.

···• ⊙ •···

You and I are the force for transformation in the world. We are the consciousness that will define the nature of the reality we are moving into.

···• ⊙ •···

Serve to relieve human suffering wherever you find it, in any way you can. Whatever your skills or karmic predicament are, there's always an opportunity to alleviate human suffering. The major way you relieve human suffering is by becoming a conscious being, and then all the rest of your stuff should also be involved in relieving human suffering in other beings.

The enlightened being, or the person that's awakened, realizes that the game is to walk through the path and leave no footprint. Leave no footprint because whatever footprint you leave is just more karmic stuff.

···• ◉ •···

I would suggest that most people find something that needs help, and then help it. Then you work on yourself to make it a conscious act. You're driven to work on yourself all the time so that your acts of caring for other human beings aren't toxic. If you want to be in a peaceful world, you damn well better be peaceful, because if you are full of anger, you are not going to bring about much peace. The qualities in yourself determine what qualities are in the world.

···• ◉ •···

If you accept that the ends of your actions often prove unknowable, you're also freer to be focused on the process of your work as it's happening. You can be attentive to situations as they occur. Helping is right here. Not having to know so badly, not wandering off looking, you're more able to be present, freer simply to be.

You needn't be troubled or worn down, then, by paradox and ambiguity. The mystery of helping can be your ally, your teacher, an environment for wonder and discovery. If you enter into it openly, your actions fall into perspective, a larger pattern you can trust. At rest in the witness, meanwhile, you greet the outcome of your work with equanimity.

···● ◙ ●···

Here is a final shift in perspective that can help release you from burnout: Do what you can.

CHAPTER 11

AWAKENING FROM CLINGING AND ATTACHMENT

*The transformative process
is our job, so that we are
not ruled by fear but by love.*

EXPLORING THE QUALITIES
OF AN ENLIGHTENED BEING

When you are in harmony with the way everything proceeds from everything else, you cannot act wrongly. Not only are you in tune with the particular act you are doing in terms of time, but in all of the ways that act is related to everything in the universe. It is a level of awareness from which actions are manifest that have no clinging, not even clinging to the effects of the act. You are not holding on anywhere. You're right here, always in the new existential moment. Moment to moment, it's a new mind. You just keep giving up your story line.

···• ⊙ •···

Interestingly, the purer one's heart becomes, the more the tiniest act resonates to bring a deeper harmony, a deeper way back into the Tao—as if one never left it.

···• ⊙ •···

When faith is strong enough, it is sufficient simply to be. It's a journey towards simplicity, towards quietness, towards a kind of joy that is not in time. It's a journey that takes you from primary identification with your body and psyche to an identification with God and ultimately beyond identification.

···• ⊙ •···

Being conscious is cutting through your own melodrama and being right here. Exist in no-mind, be empty, here now, and trust that as a situation arises, out of you will come what is necessary to deal with that situation, including the use of your intellect when appropriate. You need not continuously hold on to your intellect to reassure yourself that you know where you're at, out of fear of loss of control.

Ultimately, when you stop identifying so much with your physical body and with your psychological entity, that anxiety starts to disintegrate. You start to define yourself as in flow with the universe, and whatever comes along—death, life, joy, sadness—is grist for the mill of awakening.

···• ◎ •···

If you're going to be free, you're going to be free about the preoccupation with your worldly conditions. It doesn't mean you won't notice them, it doesn't mean you won't try to optimize them. The question is: How much emotional, attached mind are you investing in optimizing them?

HONORING YOUR INCARNATION AS YOU EVOLVE FROM ROLE TO SOUL

At some point, awakening begins.

The awakening happens with trauma, or it happens when somebody you love dies. In sexuality, you transcend separateness. It can be drugs, it can be meditation, it can be a hymn, it can be a leaf falling, it can be lying under the stars, it can be trying to solve a problem where your mind gets so one-pointed it goes through the veil. Whatever it is, you open up into other planes of consciousness that have been there in all of their splendor all the time.

·•·• ⓞ •·•·

The basic transformation that occurs—and this is the big one—is that up until a certain moment, your self-definition involves your profession, your sex, your responsibilities, and your social/cultural roles. So if anybody says, "Who are you?" you say, "I'm a lawyer; I'm a father; I'm a husband . . ."

Once this process starts to evolve, you begin to realize that the only thing you *are* is a being evolving towards full consciousness, coming into the spirit. You can use whatever metaphor you want. An awakening being. And all the rest of it is the supportive cast. All the rest of it is the stuff through which this is going on.

·•·• ⓞ •·•·

Once you understand what awakening is about,
every act of your life becomes a vehicle to
become aware, and the meaning of life changes.

·•·• ⓞ •·•·

You are awakening, or being forced to awaken, as the conditions ripen for it. This has to do with recognizing that you exist both as an actor and as a doer. As a body, personality, and as a story line. With awareness, there is a clear sense of the present.

·•·• ⓞ •·•·

If you can imagine a wheel whose rim is the cycle of births and deaths, all of the "stuff" of life, conditioned reality, and whose center is the source, you've got one foot with most of your weight on the circumference of the wheel and one foot tentatively on the center. That's the beginning of awakening. You sit down and meditate, and suddenly there's a moment when you feel the perfection of your being and your connection. Then your weight goes back on the outside of the wheel. This happens over and over and over.

Slowly, slowly the weight shifts. Then the weight shifts just enough so that there is a slight predominance on the center of the wheel, and you find that you naturally want to sit down and be quiet. You don't have to say, "I've got to meditate now," or "I've got to read a holy book," or "I've got to turn off the television set," or "I've got to do . . ." anything. It doesn't become that kind of discipline anymore. The balance has shifted.

If you keep allowing your life to become more and more simple, more and more harmonious, the less and less you grab at this and push that away.

···• ◉ •···

Ours is a journey toward simplicity, toward quietness, toward a kind of joy that is not in time. In this journey out of time to "NowHere," you leave behind every model you have had of who you thought you were.

This journey involves transforming your being so that your thinking mind becomes your servant rather than your master. It's a journey that takes you from primary identification with your psyche to identification with your soul, then to identification with God, and ultimately beyond any identification at all.

Life is an incredible curriculum in which you live richly and passionately as a way of awakening to the deepest truths of our being.

····· ◎ ·····

As a soul, I have only one motive: to merge with God. As a soul, I live in the moment, in each rich and precious moment, and I am filled with contentment.

····· ◎ ·····

You exist on many planes simultaneously at this moment. The only reason you don't know of your other identities is because you're so attached to this one. But this one or that one, don't get lost, don't stick anywhere. It's just more stuff. Go for broke—awake totally.

····· ◎ ·····

For my spiritual work, I had to hear what Alan Watts used to say to me: "Ram Dass, God is these forms. God isn't just formless. You're too addicted to formlessness." I had to learn that. I had to honor my incarnation. I've got to honor what it means to be a man, a Jew, an American, a member of the world, and a member of the ecological community. I have to figure out how to do that—how to be in my family and honor my father. All of that is part of it.

That is the way I come to God, by acknowledging my uniqueness. That's an interesting turnabout in a way. That brings spiritual people back into the world.

····· ◎ ·····

The dance goes from realizing that you're separate (which is the awakening) and then trying to find your way back into the totality of which you are not only a part, but you are.

····· ⊙ ·····

What is common to all forms is not another form. What is common to all forms is choiceless awareness; it is pure love; it is flow and harmony with the universe. It is the absence of clinging. How does it all come together? If you follow all of the forms to the apex, you are pushed beyond form and into the moment. The passing show of forms, being created and existing, then disappearing into formlessness.

····· ⊙ ·····

To see through the veil of your senses and thinking mind to the true Self often feels like humanity's highest aspiration. When you do this, it's as if you find your rightful place in the order of things. You begin to recognize a harmony that's been waiting for you to feel, and once you do this, it's not only for the life hereafter or some abstract thing for later, it's for now, for how you live your life day by day.

YOU ARE ON AN INEVITABLE COURSE OF AWAKENING

It's a little like the image of a caterpillar—enclosing itself in a cocoon in order to go through the metamorphosis to emerge as a butterfly. The caterpillar doesn't say, "Well now. I'm going to climb into this cocoon and come out a butterfly." It's just an inevitable process.

It's inevitable. It's just happening. It's got to happen that way.

You are on an inevitable course of awakening. If you deeply understand that message, it allows you to enter into your spiritual practices from a different perspective, one of patience and timelessness. You do your practices not out of a sense of duty or because you think you should, but because you know in your soul there really is nothing else you would rather do.

In Sanskrit, this is called *vairagya*, a state of weariness with worldly desire where only the desire for spiritual fulfillment is left. The spiritual pull is the last desire, one that really grabs you, but that dissolves on its own because you dissolve in the process. The Tao says, "In the end, you will be like the valley which is the favorite resort of the Way." You become receptive, become soft, become open, become attuned, become quiet. You become the ocean of love.

There is a lovely story of a boy who goes to a Zen master and asks, "Master, I know you have many students, but if I study harder than all the rest of them, how long will it take me to get enlightened?"

The master said, "Ten years."

The boy said, "Well, if I work day and night and double my efforts, how long will it take?"

The master said, "Twenty years."

Now the boy spoke of further achievement, and the master said, "Thirty years."

The boy replied, "Why do you keep adding years?"

The master answered, "Since you will have one eye on the goal, there will only be one eye left to have on the work. And it will slow you down immeasurably.

···● ◎ ●···

The cosmic humor is that if you desire to move mountains and continue to purify yourself, you will ultimately arrive at the place where you can move mountains. But to arrive at this position of power, you will have had to give up being *he-who-wanted-to-move-mountains* so that you can be *he-who-put-the-mountain-there-in-the-first-place*. The humor is that when you finally have the power to move the mountain, you are the person who placed it there—so there the mountain stays.

CHAPTER 12

PRACTICING COMPASSION IN ACTION

*I myself stand in need of the
arms of my own kindness.*

FINDING THE COURAGE TO WORK ON YOURSELF, COMPASSIONATELY

To live consciously, you must have the courage to go inside yourself to find out who you really are and understand that behind all the masks of individual differences, you are a being of beauty, love, and awareness.

When Christ said, "The kingdom of heaven is within," he wasn't just putting you on. When Buddha said, "Each person is the Buddha," he was saying the same thing. Until you can allow your own beauty, your own dignity, your own being, you cannot free another.

So if I were giving people one instruction, I would say work on yourself. Have compassion for yourself. Allow yourself to be beautiful, and all the rest will follow.

···· ◎ ····

You and I are in training to be conscious and compassionate in the truest, deepest sense—not romantically compassionate, but deeply compassionate. To be able to be an instrument of equanimity, an instrument of joy, presence, love, and availability, and at the same moment, absolutely quiet.

···· ◎ ····

Getting straight not only applies to people but things as well, such as favorite music, disliked foods, special treats, avoided places, all your toys, etc. Everything must be run through your compassion machine.

····◎····

The three levels of compassionate action that I see are: You do compassionate action as best you can as an exercise on yourself to come closer to God, to spirit, to awareness, to One. Next is you start to appreciate that you're a part of something larger than yourself, and you are an instrument of God. No longer are you doing it to get there, you're now doing it as an instrument. Third is where you lose self-consciousness, and you are God manifest. You're part of the hand of God. Then you're not doing anything. It's just God manifest.

How do you get to that third one? By honoring others and being patient.

····◎····

Acting with compassion is not "doing good" because you think you ought to. It is being drawn to action by heartfelt passion. It is giving yourself into what you are doing, being present in the moment—no matter how difficult, sad, or even boring it feels, no matter how much it demands. It is acting from your most profound understanding of what life is, listening intently for the skillful means in each situation, and not compromising the truth. It is selflessly working with others in a spirit of mutual respect.

····◎····

Some of the beings around you every day are very ancient beings, and some are very new. But is it better or worse? It's just different. Is it better to be twenty years old than fifty? It's just different. So why do

135

you judge someone because he's not as conscious as you are? Do you judge a prepubescent because he or she is not sexually aware? You understand. You have compassion.

Compassion is leaving other people alone. You don't lay trips. You exist as a statement of your own level of evolution. You are available to any human being, to provide what they need to the extent that they ask. But you begin to see that it is a fallacy to think that you can impose a trip on another person.

···• ◎ •···

When you have the compassion that comes from understanding how it is, you don't lay a trip on anybody else as to how they ought to be. You don't say to your parents, "Why don't you understand the spirit and why I'm a vegetarian?" You don't say to your husband or wife, "Why do you still want sex when all I want to do is read *The Gospel of Sri Ramakrishna*?"

A conscious being does all that he or she can to create a space for being with God but does no violence to the existing *karma* to do it.

BECOMING AN INSTRUMENT
OF COMPASSION

Bearing the unbearable is the deepest root of compassion in the world. When you bear what you think you cannot bear, who you think you are dies. You become compassion. You don't *have* compassion—you *are* compassion. True compassion goes beyond empathy to being with the experience of another. You become an instrument of compassion.

···• ◎ •···

Having empathy for another means your heart is breaking because you understand the intensity of their experience, and at the same moment, you are absolutely present. You are not clinging to anything, just watching the phenomena of the universe change. It's then that your acts can be compassionate.

The root of compassion is not empathy; that's along the lines of kindness, and that's good, but it's not compassion. Ultimate compassion is the act itself, which can relieve every level of suffering, not just the food in the belly, or the mattress to sleep on at night safely. The suffering that comes from separateness is only relieved when you are present with another person.

···· ◎ ····

The first being one must have compassion for is oneself. You can't be a witness to your thoughts with a chip on your shoulder or an axe to grind. Ramana Maharshi said, "If people would stop wailing alas, I am a sinner, and use all that energy to get on with it, they would all be enlightened." He also said, "When you're cleaning up the outer temple before going to the inner temple, don't stop to read everything you're going to throw away."

···· ◎ ····

The left hand is caught and the right hand pulls it out. The left hand turns to the right and says, "thank you." It doesn't work because they are both part of the same body. Who are you thanking? You're thanking yourself. So on that plane you realize it's not *her* suffering, *his* suffering, or *their* suffering. You go up one level, it's our suffering. You go up another level, it's my suffering. Then as it gets depersonalized, it's *the* suffering. Out of the identity with the suffering comes compassion. It arises in relationship to the suffering. It's part and parcel of the whole package. There is nothing personal in this at all.

In that sense, you have *become* compassion instead of doing compassionate acts. Instead of being compassionate, you *are* compassion.

THE GIFTS OF COMPASSIONATE ACTION

Compassionate action allows you to wake up to some of your motives and to act with more freedom. It gives you the chance to put yourself out on the edge, and if you are willing to take a clean look at what you see there, you can come to know yourself better. You can't change what is arising at any moment, because you can't change your past and your childhood. But when you stop being a stranger to yourself, you increase the number of ways you can respond to what arises.

···• ◉ •···

You see people through the veil of the fear-driven paranoia that comes from getting trapped in your separateness; when you break out of that, you experience compassion that is not pity and not kindness; but compassion born of identifying with the people around you.

···• ◉ •···

Compassionate action is a path
on which you grow in awareness and insight.
As you grow, you become a purer instrument
for change. You become a hollow reed
for the healing music of life.

••• ⊙ •••

A persistent trap all along the path is pride in your spiritual purity. It's a form of one-upmanship in which you judge others out of a feeling of superiority. This ultimately limits your spiritual awakening. You can see many people caught in this trap of virtue—for example, in the self-righteousness of some churchgoers. In the yoga scene in America, there are many groups of people who dress a certain way, eat a certain way, are special in some way that gives them an ego-enhancing feeling of purity.

The harmful effect of this trap is not so much to your social relationships—though they may become strained from this display of subtle arrogance—but rather the impact on yourself. This feeling of specialness or superiority inflates the ego and feeds it with pride. The best antidote to pride is humility, which leads to compassion.

The sooner one develops compassion in this journey, the better. Compassion lets you appreciate that each individual is doing what he or she must do and that there is no reason to judge another person or yourself. Merely do what you can to further your own awakening.

CHAPTER 13

LIVING IN LOVING AWARENESS

I myself stand in need of the arms of my own kindness.

LOVE IS A STATE OF BEING

The object of your love is love itself. It is the inner light in everyone and everything. Love is a state of being. You begin to love people because they just are. You see the mystery of the Divine in form. When you live in love, you see love everywhere you look. You are literally in love with everyone you look at.

When you and I rest together in loving awareness, we swim together in the ocean of love. Remember, it's always right here. Enter into the flow of love with a quiet mind and see all things as a part of yourself.

···• ◎ •···

When two people meet in the space of love and break the attachment of the mind, seeing the other person as the vehicle to get you there, you realize that it's in you, and through your spiritual practices you start to rest in it.

Suddenly the need and desperation begin to dissolve. All of the negative things that go with addiction begin to disappear—the possessiveness, the jealousy, the anger, the frustration, the fear that the other person's going to die—because the quality of love as a state has no time, it has no space. It wasn't born, and it doesn't die.

···• ◎ •···

When you see the Beloved all around you, everyone is family and everywhere is love. When I allow myself to see the beauty of another being and see the inherent beauty of soul manifesting itself, I feel the quality of love in that being's presence. It doesn't matter what we're doing. We could be talking about our cats because we happen to be picking out cat food in the supermarket, or we could be simply passing each other on the sidewalk.

When you are being love, you extend an environment outward that allows others to act in different, more loving, more peaceful ways than they are used to behaving. Not only does it let them be more loving, but it also encourages them to be so.

···• ⊙ •···

Love is abundant because you are love. As you become love, you get to the point where you walk down the street, and someone comes, and it is the most beautiful thing that you have ever seen. You look and appreciate and love, your eyes meet, you both recognize the love, and you don't have to do anything about it. It's nothing special to be in love; it's very ordinary. How alien it is in this culture to think that being in love with the universe is ordinary.

···• ⊙ •···

Each of us is separate, yet each of us is part of the whole, but sometimes you get lost a bit in dualism, and then you find your way back out. Every time you find yourself in unconditional love, you remember that we are all one. When you remember, you open. And when you open, love pours through you.

If you became a person who could love unconditionally, everyone you loved would flower before your very eyes, and everywhere you looked would be light. That's one of the fringe benefits of bhakti yoga. It's breathtaking at every moment.

···• ⊙ •···

Contentment is an attitude of the soul rather than the ego or personality. You look at life from what I call the soul plane. Love and compassion are emotions that arise from the soul. When you identify with your soul, you live in a loving universe. The soul loves everybody. It's like the sun. It brings out the beauty in each of us. You can feel it in your heart.

···• ⊙ •···

What love has been for me has been the whole "heart" part of my journey. I have gone from having special people that I loved and others that I hated to realizing that everybody I meet is the "beloved" in drag. Everybody is "the One." My job is to see through the story line their mind is caught in, not to reject the story line, not to judge it; it's not any better or worse than my story line. It's about not getting caught in it and being able to see what is behind it.

It's behind the soul, and because you can't talk about it, touch it, smell it, taste it, you tend to think it doesn't exist, and yet here you are—that's the beautiful perplexity of it all.

LOVE IS NOT A CURRENCY MEANT FOR EXCHANGE

The most important aspect of love is not in giving or receiving; it's in the being. When I need love from others or need to give love to others, I'm caught in an unstable situation. Being in love—rather than giving or taking love—is the only thing that provides stability. Being in love means seeing the Beloved all around me.

···• ⊙ •···

Since love is a state of being, and a divine state at that, the state to which we all yearn to return, we wish to possess love. At best, you can try to possess the key to your heart, your Beloved, but sooner or later, you find that even that is impossible. To possess the key is to lose it.

···• ⊙ •···

Unconditional love exists in each of us.
It is part of our deep inner being. It is not
so much an active emotion as a state of being.
It's not, "I love you" for this or that reason,
not "I love you if you love me."
It's love for no reason, love without an object.

···• ⊙ •···

You are loved just for being who you are, just for existing. You don't have to do anything to earn it. Your shortcomings, lack of self-esteem, physical imperfection, or social and economic success—none of that matters. No one can take this love away from you, and it will always be here. Imagine that being in this love is like relaxing endlessly into a warm bath that surrounds and supports your every movement, so that every thought and feeling is permeated by it. You feel as though you are dissolving into love.

···• ⊙ •···

Love doesn't know boundaries. The mind creates the boundary of separation between you and me. The heart keeps embracing and opening out so that things that open your heart open you out into the universe and allow you to experience preciousness, the grace, the sweetness, and the thick interconnectedness of it all. It's more than interconnected. It's all one thing, and it keeps changing its flow and patterns, and you're a part of it.

·· • • 🔘 • • ··

This is the path of love, the path of the heart. Like all paths, it is fraught with pitfalls and traps, and most of your emotions are either in the service of your mind or frightening things that overwhelm you and make you afraid, so you protect yourself from them. So you come through life a little bit like a hungry ghost. We are beings that have huge needs for love, but seemingly it's like we have some amoeba that doesn't allow us to digest our food. So, though you get love, it goes through you, and then you need love all over again.

This conception is so deep within all of us that you've built an entire reality around it, and you think that's the way it is; that everybody needs love and that if you don't get it, you are deprived, and that the more of it, the better, and you need it every day from everything.

·· • • 🔘 • • ··

Maharajji said to me, "Ram Dass, love everybody." And I said, "I can't do it." He said it again—love everybody—but then I realized it had to do with the soul and not the ego, because the ego judges, but the soul loves everybody because everybody is a soul and a soul loves another soul. It's not that the small, limited, ego "I" loves you, but it's unconditional love, it comes from the ocean of infinite love.

"I AM LOVING AWARENESS"

You can get to the place of being loving awareness, but before you can love the universe or other people, you have to be able to love yourself. That love throws you into the next plane, which I call the soul plane. It is spiritual, but it also deals with separation, because the soul wants to meld with the One. The One is love, light; the One is peace, compassion. The soul wants to meld with that.

···• ◉ •···

If I go into the place in myself that is love,
and you go into the place in yourself that is love,
we are together in love. Then you and I are truly in love,
the state of being love. That's the entrance to Oneness.
That's the space I entered when I met my guru.

···• ◉ •···

When you are experiencing fear, you are caught in your separateness. When you are experiencing love, you are caught in your unity with all things. Love, the verb "love," is a vehicle of permeating boundaries. You feel the quality of love, which means a flow of energy or merging with the universe. That is the antidote to fear. It's going to the place behind your separateness.

···• ◉ •···

This love is actually part of you, it is always flowing through you. It's like the subatomic texture of the universe, the dark matter that connects everything. When you tune into that flow, you will feel it in your heart—not your physical heart or your emotional heart, but your spiritual heart, the place you point to in your chest when you say, *"I am."*

···· ⦿ ····

When you can learn to accept love, you can give love. You can give love to all you perceive, all the time. *I am loving awareness.* You can be aware of your eyes seeing, your ears hearing, your skin feeling, and your mind producing thoughts, thought after thought. Thoughts are seductive, but you don't have to identify with them. You identify not with the thoughts, but with the awareness of the thoughts. To bring loving awareness to everything, you turn your awareness to be love. This moment is love.

···· ⦿ ····

Most of us identify with our awareness through the ego, through the mind and senses. But the true Self is in the middle of our chest, in your spiritual heart. So, to get from ego to the true Self, I said, "I am loving awareness." Loving awareness is the soul. I am loving awareness. I am aware of everything, I'm aware of my body and my senses and my mind, I'm aware of all of it, but I notice that I'm loving all of it. I'm loving all of the world.

···· ⦿ ····

How does one become loving awareness?

If I change my identification from the ego to the soul, then as I look at people, they all appear like souls. I turn from my head, the thought of who I am, to my spiritual heart, which is a different sort of awareness—feeling directly, intuiting, loving awareness. It's changing from a worldly outer identification to an inner spiritual identification. Concentrate on your spiritual heart, right in the middle of your chest. Keep repeating the phrase, *"I am loving awareness. I am loving awareness."*

CHAPTER 14

APPROACHING DEATH WITH LESS FEAR AND MORE CURIOSITY

*If I'm going to die, the best way
to prepare is to quiet my mind
and open my heart.
If I'm going to live, the best way
to prepare is to quiet my mind
and open my heart.*

REMAINING PRESENT DURING LIFE'S LAST CHAPTERS

The stroke has given me another way to serve people. It lets me feel more deeply the pain of others; to help them know by example that ultimately, whatever happens, no harm can come. "Death is perfectly safe," I like to say.

·••• ◎ •••·

In aging, our minds are often permeated by memories of the past or worries about the future. What gets missed is the present—and right there in the moment is the doorway into timelessness. When you are fully present in the moment, there is no anticipatory fear or anxiety because you are here and now, not in the future. When you are resting in your soul, death is just closing a chapter in a book.

·••• ◎ •••·

Death is our greatest challenge, as well as our greatest spiritual opportunity. By cultivating mindfulness, you can prepare yourself for this final passage by allowing nature, rather than ego, to guide you. In so doing, you become a teacher to others, and your own best friend, looking beyond the body's death at the next stage in your soul's adventure.

·••• ◎ •••·

The way you regard death is critical
to the way you experience life.
When your fear of death changes,
the way you live your life changes.

···• ◎ •···

Open and stay centered. If you remain centered, your calm presence helps to free all those around you. Go inside yourself to that quiet place where you are wisdom. Wisdom has in it compassion. Compassion understands about life and death. The answer to death is to be present in the moment.

···• ◎ •···

One dies as one lives. What else can better prepare you to die than the way you live? The game is to be where you are—honestly, consciously, and as fully as you know how. Once you have awakened, you can't fully go back to sleep.

Regardless of what happens in the world, I'm still going to follow Maharajji's instructions every day—to love everyone, serve everyone, and remember God.

···• ◎ •···

Part of your curriculum with aging is to shift
your game to honor the systems of which
you're a part so that you finish your work
on Earth. In other words, you get free.

···• ◎ •···

Our human forms are composed of an infinite myriad of forms, all in constant motion, from the subatomic to the cosmic in scale. This is the *lila*, the enchanted dance of existence, the divine interplay of consciousness and energy. Amid this divine play, seek fulfillment, perfection, flow, freedom, enlightenment, Oneness.

The dominant quality of form is change because all forms are in time. That's another way of saying we don't know what will happen from one instant to another. One of my guru brothers is fond of saying, "Don't be surprised to be surprised!" For instance, I didn't anticipate I'd be living in a wheelchair. The way to live with change is to be completely present in the moment (remember, Be Here Now).

···• ◎ •···

How would I like to enter my own death?
With a feeling of, I don't know, but wow!
It's going to be interesting.

···• ◎ •···

I've begun to expand my awareness to be able to look at the universe as it is, and see what is called the horrible beauty. I mean, there's horror and beauty in all of it, because there is also decay and death. We're all decaying—I look at my hand and it's decaying. It's beautiful and horrible at the same time, and I live with that. I see and live with the beauty of it. So we're talking about appreciating what is.

···• ◎ •···

My work around the issue of aging is to quiet the mind—standing back enough so that I am not so caught in the culture and the set of attitudes I developed from my childhood. I can see what is and respond in harmony with that, to become a part of it, which is the way a bird sings or a river flows or a baby cries.

···• ◎ •···

When I meditate I sit quietly, I withdraw the awareness of my ears hearing, my eyes seeing. I don't move around much. I sit quietly and I go deep inside. What happens when you grow old? You lose your hearing, and you lose your sight, you can't move around very much—what an ideal time for doing inner work!

Aging has its own beauty. You have a chance not to be so dependent on social approval. You can be a little more eccentric. You can be more alone. And you can examine loneliness and boredom instead of being afraid of them. There is such an art and a possibility in aging.

THE IMPORTANCE OF LEARNING TO GRIEVE

Death is very much a part of life, and it has cycles like leaves falling in autumn. It has touch, taste, sound, feeling. Think about being in a culture where death is not seen as a failure or an enemy, but as a stage of life.

···• ◎ •···

While the crisis stage of grief does pass in its own time—and each person's grief has its own timetable—deep feelings don't disappear completely. But ultimately, you come to the truth of the adage that "love is stronger than death."

I once met with a woman whose boyfriend was killed in Central America. She was grieving, and it was paralyzing her life. I characterized it for her this way: "Let's say you're in 'wise-woman training.'" If she's in wise-woman training, everything in her life must be grist for the mill. Her relationship with this man would become part of the wisdom in her. But first, she had to see that her relationship with him is between souls. They no longer have two incarnated bodies to share, so she had to find the soul connection. Two souls can access each other without an incarnation.

···• ◎ •···

In working with those who are dying, I offer another human being a spacious environment with my mind in which they can die as they need to die. I have no right to define how another person should die. I'm just there to help them transition, however they need to do it.

···• ◎ •···

I am often dealing with people who have lost someone who has died, and they are grieving. What they are really grieving for is their connection to the place in themselves where they feel safe in the universe and at home and at love and at peace. They have so identified it with the other person, with an external thing, that they are absolutely destitute and feel like they have lost the juice of life.

It is like a meditator who can't meditate. It's the same addiction. You get so busy you can't stop in the morning to sit, and you start to feel like you've lost your Beloved; you've lost that place of your being. I encourage people to stay with what they are feeling, with their grief, and I always tell people, "How long have you grieved?" and they'll say, "Oh, a year." I'll say, "Oh, grieve some more."

See, the culture says, "Well, it's good you're over it now. Now you can start living life again." But grieving has to run its course. Those are very deep attachments, and you go up and go down. You think, "I've broken out," and then the next moment you've crashed into depression, and on it goes.

····◎····

It is important, as you get older, to learn how to grieve. Although this may sound self-evident, experience has taught me that it is not. In a culture that emphasizes stoicism and forward movement, time is deemed "of the essence," and there is little tolerance for slowness, inwardness, and melancholy. Grieving—a healthy, necessary aspect of life—is too often overlooked.

Over the years in working with grieving people, I've encouraged them first of all to surrender to the experience of their pain. To counteract the natural tendency to turn away from pain, open to it as fully as possible and allow their heart to break.

You must take enough time to remember your losses—be they friends or loved ones who have passed away, the death of long-held hopes or dreams, the loss of homes, careers, or countries, or health you may never get back again. Rather than close yourself to grief, it helps to realize that you only grieve for what you love.

····◎····

The way you deal with grief has a lot to do with whether or not the grief heals and strengthens you, or ends up depriving and starving you. We've learned many things about grief over the years, like that strong "grin and bear it," stiff-upper-lip response to grief, which involves denial, is not an optimal strategy for dealing with a mourning period. There is a reaction to a loss that is a grieving process, and you need to deal with the grieving in a way that is true to your being. It's just as untrue to grieve when you're not feeling it as it is to not grieve when you're feeling it.

My reaction to grieving people is to give them a lot of support in grieving and let the process run its course. That means not only the grief of the loss of the person, but also the grief of the loss of any dream in life, the loss of anything that you've invested yourself in.

DISTINGUISHING YOUR SOULS FROM YOURSELF

Spiritual practices help you move from identifying with the ego to identifying with the soul. Old age does that for you, too. It spiritualizes people naturally.

Aging gives you a chance to learn to use the shadows in your life as vehicles for your awakening—and the longest shadow of all is death. How you relate to death is the key spiritual work of aging. And how you see death is a function of how much you identify with that which dies. Egos die. Souls don't die.

•••• ◎ ••••

As you identify more with the soul,
fear dissipates, and trust grows,
because the soul is not afraid of death.

···• ⊙ •···

Ramana Maharshi was a great Indian saint. When he was dying of cancer, his devotees said, "Let's treat it." Ramana Maharshi said, "No, it is time to drop this body." His devotees started to cry. They begged him, "*Bhagwan*, don't leave us, don't leave us!" He looked at them with confusion and said, "Don't be silly. Where could I possibly go?"

You know, it's almost like he was saying, "Don't make such a fuss. I'm just selling the old family car." These bodies we live in, and the ego that identifies with it, are like the old family car. They are functional entities in which our soul travels through our incarnation. When they are used up, they die.

The most graceful thing to do is to allow them to die peacefully and naturally—to "let go lightly." Through it all, who you are is a soul. And when the body and the ego are gone, the soul will live on, because the soul is eternal. Eventually, in some incarnation, when you've finished your work, your soul can merge back into the One, into God, into the infinite. In the meantime, your soul uses bodies, egos, and personalities to work through the karma of each incarnation.

···• ⊙ •···

Working to accept death does not exclude efforts to heal the body. In other words, you can swim with the dolphins, have chemotherapy or radiation, or whatever, if simultaneously you are also working on death so that you can keep the balance even. "Ah, death. Ah, life." That's the optimal place. Not, "I wish for death" or "I'm going towards death." Also, not, "I must have life" or "I can't possibly have death." It's the aversion or attraction that is the root of suffering, which turns into a problem at the moment of death.

···• ⊙ •···

People ask me if I believe there is continuity after death. I say that I don't believe it—it just is. This offends my scientific friends to no end. But belief is something you hold with your intellect, and for me, this goes way beyond my intellect.

The *Bhagavad Gita* tells us, "As the Spirit of our mortal body wanders on in childhood and youth and old age, the Spirit wanders on to a new body; of this, the sage has no doubts." As Krishna says, "Because we all have been for all time . . . And we all shall be for all time, forever and ever."

···• ⊙ •···

When my biological mother was dying in a hospital in Boston in 1966, I would watch all the people come into her room. All of the doctors and relatives would say, "You are looking better, you are doing well." Then they would go out of the room and say, "She won't last a week." I thought how bizarre it was that a human being could be going through one of the most profound transitions in their life, and have everyone they know and love and trust lying to them.

Can you hear the pain of that? No one could be straight with my mother because everyone was too frightened. Even the rabbi. She and I talked about it, and she said, "What do you think death is?" I said, "I don't know, Mother. But I look at you, and you are my friend, and it looks like you are in a building that is burning down, but you are still here. I suspect when the building burns entirely, it will be gone, but you will still be here." So my mother and I met in that space.

···• ⊙ •···

The only thing that ever dies
is the model you have in your mind
of who you think you are.

···• ⊙ •···

I've often been struck by the poignancy of meeting older people of great wealth and power and seeing how frightened they are of losing what they have. The greater their clinging, the greater their pain, realizing how little use the accouterments of power and worldly position are in helping them age with wisdom and peace.

In truth, the ego's attachment to power of any kind is linked inextricably to the fear of losing that power, and thus becomes a source of suffering. There is a kind of power that does not give rise to fear, however. It is spiritual power, the power of the enlightened mind. As you begin to emphasize soul power over worldly power, your perception of the alterations brought on by aging changes proportionately.

···• ⊙ •···

There's no clinging to that which dies. For who you are, were, and will be, these are simply processes of transformation. Just like it's hard for a prepubescent to understand that a time will come when his baseball cards aren't that relevant, so the time will come when even your mortal coil is not that relevant.

····• ◎ •····

Old age is rife with change. It's training you in change: change in your body, in relationships, your energy, your role.

The last part of your life is sensational. *Yum, yum, yum.*

Ego things calm down and wisdom comes forth. And compassion comes forth—compassion for yourself, for others, for the world.

Honoring Ram Dass into the
future and spreading his wisdom
to all seekers far and wide

ABOUT RAM DASS

In 1967, Ram Dass was still Dr. Richard Alpert, a prominent Harvard psychologist and psychedelic pioneer with Dr. Timothy Leary. He continued his psychedelic research until he took a fateful trip to India later that year. In India, he met his guru, Neem Karoli Baba, who gave him the Hindu name Ram Dass, which means "servant of God." Everything changed then—his intense dharmic life started, and he became a pivotal influence on a culture that has reverberated with the words "Be Here Now" ever since. Ram Dass's spirit has been a guiding light for several generations.

From 1968 onward, Ram Dass pursued a panoramic array of spiritual methods and practices from ancient wisdom traditions including Buddhist meditation in the Theravadin, Mahayana Tibetan, and Zen Buddhist schools, and Sufi and Jewish mystical studies. He also practiced and taught bhakti yoga—which focuses on devotion and the Hindu deity Hanuman. Perhaps most significantly, his practice of karma yoga or spiritual service has opened up millions of other souls to their deep, yet individuated spiritual practice and path.

Ram Dass passed away at his home on Maui on December 22, 2019.

About the Love Serve Remember Foundation

The Love Serve Remember Foundation is dedicated to preserving and continuing the teachings of Ram Dass and his guru Neem Karoli Baba. The foundation facilitates the continuation of these teachings through retreats, online courses and events, blog content, films, podcasts, social network channels, and collaborative projects with conscious artists and musicians.

To find out more about Ram Dass and his teachings, visit www.ramdass.org and beherenownetwork.com.

MANDALA

An imprint of MandalaEarth
PO Box 3088, San Rafael, CA 94912
www.MandalaEarth.com

PUBLISHER: Raoul Goff
ASSOCIATE PUBLISHER: Phillip Jones
VP OF CREATIVE: Chrissy Kwasnik
VP OF MANUFACTURING: Alix Nicholaeff
ASSOCIATE ART DIRECTOR: Ashley Quackenbush
SENIOR PRODUCTION MANAGER: Greg Steffen
SENIOR PRODUCTION MANAGER, SUBSIDIARY RIGHTS: Lina s Palma

RAM DASS
LOVE SERVE REMEMBER
Foundation

COMPILED BY Rachael Fisher
EDITED BY Christopher Fiorello & Parvati Markus
COVER AND BOOK DESIGN BY HR Hegnauer

ISBN: 978-1-64722-487-5

Library of Congress Cataloging-in-Publication Data is available upon request.

ROOTS of PEACE   REPLANTED PAPER

Mandala Publishing, in association with Roots of Peace, will plant two trees for each tree used in the manufacturing of this book. Roots of Peace is an internationally renowned humanitarian organization dedicated to eradicating land mines worldwide and converting war-torn lands into productive farms and wildlife habitats. Roots of Peace will plant two million fruit and nut trees in Afghanistan and provide farmers there with the skills and support necessary for sustainable land use.

Manufactured in China by Insight Editions

10 9 8 7 6 5 4 3 2